first, a Prologue CONCERNING

... somebody once said
don't you want be an a
behind these questions
work of

> ... when you next see someone using a mobile phone - in the street or in a country lane, on a bus or a plane - go up to this person and ask 'Where are you going?' ... and if the reply is 'I'm going to my office', on no account say, 'But you are already in your office.'

a set of proposals, a set of windows through which to see a 'new world', is only a rather pathetic regurgitation of the dogma which asserts that architectural drawings are representations of something that wishes to become.[1] Archigram's efforts lay not in this tradition; they were not re-styled modernism, they represented a conceptual shift, in common with other creative enterprises, away from an interest in the commodity (in this case, say, the building or the city) towards an interest in the protocols, structures and processes of mid twentieth-century culture. One might then argue: 'why draw it so exhaustively?' — and in a sense, perhaps, the weight of the drawing does 'detract' from the content of the work.

If when it's raining on Oxford Street the buildings are no more important than the rain, why draw the buildings and not the rain? Well, I can only ask you to concentrate on the question whilst enjoying the picture – sorry, the drawing – and perhaps see the buildings as advertisements, part normative architectural rendering, part provocation, and then reconsider the fact that a building is a sort of residue, a ghostly reminder of all the ongoing processes –

1 Nomadism
   Metamorphosis
   Time
   Exchange
   Consumption
   Lifestyle
   Transience

David Greene

economic, technical and social — that make up the environment in which it was produced. In reconsidering this environment Archigram also asked that it be seen in the context of consumerism and the aesthetic and technical social systems that follow on from this. It doesn't help to over-sentimentalise here: a building is a commodity, 70 per cent of the UK population have one, which they polish, paint and restyle. Although Archigram embraced this fact with perhaps an alarming lack of critique, it was also with a boundless innocent enthusiasm. Behind all the work lies a persistent optimism in technology, pure faith in the future, and scorn poured upon the reiterations of modernist dogma — or, rather, the refusal of post-war practice to invest the modernist project with new emerging realities. This is a new terrain in which information becomes almost a substance, a new material with the power to reshape social arrangements, in which the city becomes a continuous building site in a very literal sense, in which things and people vibrate and oscillate around the globe in an ecstatic consumption of energy, in which the modernist search for the authentic is an anachronism, in which restlessness is the current cultural condition. This is the landscape inhabited by Archigram.

It would be invidious to select any one project, there are too many overlaps, but it is perhaps appropriate to try to summarise the key concepts that infest to varying degrees all the work, if only to demonstrate that these concepts are still relevant.

If we consider for a moment Christo's seminal work — the 'wrapped cliff' — we might see it in one of two ways: as a wrapped cliff or,

Prologue

preferably, as the point at which all other cliffs are unwrapped. An Archigram project attempts to achieve this same altered reading of the familiar (in the tradition of Buckminister Fuller's question, 'How much does your building weigh?'). It provides a new agenda where nomadism is the dominant social force; where time, exchange and metamorphosis replace stasis; where consumption, lifestyle and transience become the programme; and where the public realm is an electronic surface enclosing the globe.

Lodged as it was in the 1960s, Archigram's work failed to anticipate the rapid dominance of certain technical developments or issues, in particular biotechnology, nanotechnology and environmental issues. But, more noticeably, the optimism of that period gave way to Kroker's assertion that panic is the key psychological mood of the post-modern era. So can it be suggested that Archigram is a point of slippage between the modern and the post-modern, with none of the nihilism and fascination with decay and absence of the latter, yet disregarding the obsessive concern with all aspects of the authentic of the former?

Archigram is about the possibilities for architecture – the 'both/and' rather than the 'either/or' – not only with regard to speculation on architectural language and form, but also in terms of the widening of the site of conceptual interest that the architectural project might occupy and the kind of drawings (propaganda) that could be a tool of speculation.

Like its architecture, the working method for Archigram was ad hoc,

David Greene

nomadic and episodic. Archigram was not so much a group as a collection of exposed nerves/firecrackers … jumping and occasionally colliding to form even larger bangs.

So when did the fireworks end, or, if one regards current practice in the case of, say, Canary Wharf, are they still conceptually splattering? Archigram's questions concerning the technical remain unanswered, if they were ever posed, but it would seem that the electronic nomads of the global financial systems demand a permanence in their architecture that they do not require in their business.

If Archigram were wrong, then architecture cannot escape its historical mission to resist time and become, literally, an investment. It cannot become the rain; the nomad is destined to be a renegade, a vagabond; metamorphosis of form is undesirable, the wall of stone may not be the wall of light and the building may not be seen as a transient presence.

So when you next see someone using a mobile phone –
in the street or in a country lane, on a bus or a plane –
go up to this person and ask:
'Where are you going?' …
and if the reply is
'I'm going to my office',
on no account say,
'But you are already in your office.'

Prologue

Walking City in the Desert, Ron Herron 1964–73

Capsule Tower,
Warren Chalk 1964

CITIES:MOVING

Dear Ron and Warren

Although you are no longer with us in this world you are in spirit, your work is here and on the walls and your voices rattle in our minds – hopefully we are still the optimistic exposed nerves you would want us to be. Through this publication and exhibition we hear and see you and so do others. We dedicate it to you with gratitude for fantastic memories of our friendship.

David, Dennis, Peter and Spider

This publication was produced to coincide with the showing of the exhibition Archigram: Experimental Architecture 1961–74 at Cornerhouse Gallery in Manchester, England (January–March 1998), and for its tour of the United States, showing in New York at Thread Waxing Space, StoreFront for Art and Architecture and the Arthur Ross Architecture Gallery, Columbia University and at the Hartell Gallery, Cornell University, Ithaca (March–April 1998); The Art Center College of Design/Alyce de Roulet Williamson Gallery, Pasadena (August–October 1998); San Francisco Museum of Modern Art and the San Francisco Art Institute (March–June 1999); Henry Art Gallery/Fay G Allen Center for the Visual Arts, Seattle (July–October 1999).

The exhibition and this publication were designed and produced on behalf of the Archigram Group by Dennis Crompton with the help of Peter Cook, David Greene and Michael Webb, and assisted by Caroline O'Hanrahan, Annie Bridges, Catherine Crompton and Daniel Crompton. The original exhibition as shown in Vienna was conceived and designed by Ron Herron and Dennis Crompton. We are grateful to Ron's family for allowing his work to remain in the public realm.

Front cover: *the design is based on the cover of* Archigram *6 by Geoff Reeve and a book jacket designed by Warren Chalk*

First published 1998 in the United Kingdom for Cornerhouse Gallery.
Second edition published 1998 in the United States for Thread Waxing Space.
Third revised edition published 1999 by Archigram Archives.

Forth edition 2002

© 1999 Archigram Archives and the authors.

All rights reserved

The entire contents of this publication are copyright and cannot be reproduced in any manner whatsoever without written permission from the publishers.

ISBN 0 9535119 0 1

Reproduction and printing by Dexter Graphics Ltd London

Archigram Archives   38 Regents Park Road   London NW1 7SX

CONCERNING ARCHIGRAM...
edited by Dennis Crompton

Contents

1	A Prologue Concerning Archigram *David Greene*	
10	Introduction *Michael Sorkin*	
14	Archigram Entr'Acte 1 The Beginning *Peter Cook*	
18	Archigram Classic The Furniture Manufacturers Association Headquarters *Michael Webb* 1958	
25	Archigram: A Necessary Irritant *Barry Curtis*	
80	Archigram Entr'Acte 2 Capsules, Pods and Skins *Peter Cook*	
88	Archigram Classic Entertainments Centre, Leicester Square, London *Michael Webb* 1959–	
94	Archigram Classic Entertainment Tower, Montreal *Peter Cook* 1963	
98	The Notion of Motion *Michael Webb*	
106	Archigram Entr'Acte 3 Folkestone *Peter Cook*	
110	Archigram Classic Living Pod *David Greene* 1966	
114	Archigram Robots	
118	Mobile Projects	
122	Archigram Entr'Acte 4 Los Angeles *Peter Cook*	
132	Monte Carlo Three Projects	
138	Archigram Entr'Acte 5 Addhox *Peter Cook*	
140	Landscape Projects	
144	World's Last Hardware Event *David Greene*	
160	Archigram: Welcome to New York *William Menking*	

ARCHIGRAM ARCHIVES LONDON

ACKNOWLEDGEMENTS

Archigram Archives is grateful for the tireless support received from many people and organisations since 1993 when the exhibition and consequent publications first started to emerge.

The foundations for this publication were established initially by Pascal Schöning and Herbert Lachmayer, who promoted the Archigram work and secured the backing of the Kunsthalle Wien, directed by Toni Stooss. He in turn brought in the Centre Georges Pompidou, Paris, and its Architecture Curator, Alain Guiheux.

This publication became possible through the encouragement and support of Cornerhouse Gallery, Manchester and Thread Waxing Space, New York and their directors Paul Bailey and Ellen Salpeter. Thread Waxing Space were in partnership with Pratt Institute, Columbia and Cornell Universities and The StoreFront for Art and Architecture. Our thanks to Tom Hanrahan, Bernard Tschumi, Tony Vidler and Kyong Park, who represented these institutions.

Our special thanks go to Ellen Salpeter, whose endless enthusiasm maintained the tour of our work and the distribution of this publication throughout the United States.

The Archigram members are indebted to Bill Menking, Professor of Architecture and City Planning at Pratt, for his tireless support and efforts on our behalf in curating the exhibition in the USA and for his contribution to this publication. We are also grateful to Michael Sorkin and Barry Curtis for their thoughtful writing.

Archigram Archives thanks the Building Centre Trust for their advice and support and Davey Photo Summit and Advance Photoprinters for their continued help with the reproduction and preservation of our work.

The production of this publication has only been possible through the support of our printers Dexter Graphics, in the person of Keith Deal whose tolerance he has allowed us to test once again.

PREFACE

In constructing this book I very purposely put David's Prologue right at the very front so that his words were the first that you found when opening the covers. I love it. It encapsulates and summarises what Archigram is (not WAS) all about. If you arrived here without reading it, then go back, read it and pick me up later.

The last few years have seen a revived interest in the work of our group during the sixties and early seventies. A short while ago a good friend jokingly introduced me to an audience as 'a living fossil' and he had a point. Whilst some recent critics have written that our work still looks to the future (and perhaps it does but only in the sense that the present has not yet caught up with the past), you must read it in the context of its period. It is now a part of history and it is up to you to reinterpret our propositions in the present. I firmly believe that the fundamentals will always apply but they require constant reinterpretation.

My purpose in presenting some of our work in this publication is that you should be informed. The original sources are now only to be found on the dusty shelves of academic libraries and the secondary sources are incomplete and all too often factually incorrect.

One of the guiding rules of our proposals was that architecture, whether experimental or built, should bring enjoyment to those who experience it. I sincerely hope that this little book will achieve this same goal.

Dennis Crompton
London, January 1999

INTRODUCTION
Michael Sorkin

1964 was the year of the great British Invasion of America. Capped by the world historical appearance of the Beatles on the Ed Sullivan Show, a deluge of male rock groups – including not simply the Fab Four but the Rolling Stones, the Searchers, the Animals, Jerry and the Pacemakers and Herman's Hermits – took control of the charts and held on for almost a decade.

The British Invasion was in many ways the return of the repressed. In the post-Elvis years, American rock 'n roll had become anaemic and stupid, filled with Fabians and Bobby Rydells, and Elvis wannabes whose music was both saccharine and almost completely disconnected from the blues-based sources that formed the foundation for Elvis's own great leap forward. Independently, the Brits rediscovered Chuck Berry, Little Richard and earlier blues titans like Howlin' Wolf and Big Bill Broonzy, and reconstituted, electrified and transformed a tradition that we had squandered. At the same time, they Europeanised rock by introducing their own sonorities and sensibilities and opened the door for globalised production.

But rock 'n roll wasn't the only repressed restored by the Brits. In 1960, Archigram coalesced and began an inventive run that paralleled that of the Beatles, including the ultimate, amicable split and the continuation of a number of solo careers. Like the Beatles, Archigram was not founded on any clarion declaration but came together almost casually – like-minded lads with a childhood in common, a rebellious sense of purpose and a remarkable lack of rancour towards the system they sought to overturn. And, like the Beatles, Archigram sought to recover squandered themes, to re-examine sites mainstream architecture had written off, machines in the garden, the joys of consumption, the universal family of the object, the circus of ideas.

Archigram's agenda – to the degree it can be reduced – was the domestication of technology by selective appropriation and the cultivation of an architecture attuned to the swinging sixties subject. Of course, functionalism – the received architecture of the day – had advanced a structurally similar programme (even if its fantasy of subjectivity was a lot less groovy) but, because of its roots in the utopian socialist tradition, the forms it revered were those with a more specifically industrial content. Le Corbusier's famous description of the house as a 'machine for living' had something particular in mind – the efficient machines of the assembly line.

Archigram was clearly thinking about something else: Gropius could never have imagined the Cushicle. To be sure, there was a visible thrall with the big constructions of the era, the skyscrapers and moon-shots and oil-rigs. But this was leavened by another set of images which included both the boy-specific Spitfires and Meccano sets of their common childhoods and the architecture of the fun-fair with its roller coasters and parachute jumps, a highly elaborated and very refined technology of construction devoted to the production not of material goods but of pleasure. Perhaps more than any other architects, Archigram made a lunge at the parsimonious aesthetic of modernity, insisting that functionalism always begin with fun.

'Rage at the machine' was a memorable emotion of those days. Archigram shared the impulse but was anything but angry. Their protest was literally constructive, posed via a benign alternative,

Michael Sorkin

combining a hand-drawn, harmless, cartoon (a deeply affirmative medium for Archigram) megalomania (those cities walking on water) and an arcadian reverie. To Archigram, the global village was both those things and their work displayed this two-sidedness consistently. On one side there was the rhapsody of the replicable, the nominally flexible world-democracy of pods, of architecture transmuted to the status of appliance. On the other, there was the William Morrisoid suit, the delight in both the eccentricity of country life and a vast, extremely English, reservoir of sympathy with the lovingly manipulated landscape.

Archigram may have been the last great architects of the nineteenth century, collapsing two of its great impulses – the Brunelesque love of big engineering and a fantasy of the happinesses of rural life – as a double cure for the alienations of the urban. I note, in retrospect, that the Archigrammers are contemporaries of Robert Venturi, who played a learned Fabian (both senses) to the six's Beatles. While both aimed at an architecture that tapped into a vivid cultural lode, Archigram's appropriation was all innocence, drafted into service at the source, unmediated by account: they lived it. Venturi was more self-conscious, academic, touristic, filled with flat irony: he observed it. And, his architecture ultimately foundered on compromise, on the idea that pop-cultural sources needed to be transformed to find their utility, and on his own private absorption with the classical tradition, with tradition in general in the T S Eliot (that ersatz Brit) sense. Venturi wound up an astute decorator, a signifier jockey in the best post-modern sense. Archigram was never much interested in signification. They went straight from intentions to objects and let the meanings sort themselves out.

Towards the end of the sixties, Archigram's work became increasingly preoccupied with its own invisibility, with a weightless

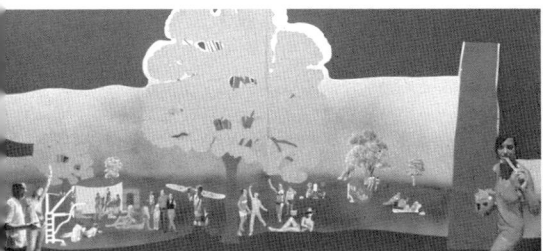

Monte Carlo Entertainments Centre (1969), surface drawn by David Greene and underground by Ron Herron

nomadology. The various manifestations of a 'bugged ground' – the Logplugs and Rokplugs and Quietly Technologised Folk Suburbias, the almost-built underground Monte Carlo Entertainment Centre, the Hedgerow Village, the Crater City, the Prepared Landscape – all symptomised a crisis in optimism that must surely have been informed by the misappropriated technology of the war in Vietnam with its own prepared landscape of the electronic battlefield and its co-optation of the romance and potential beneficence of the machine for the commission of murder. As we defoliated Asia, the movement for a more rational sense of global ecology was being born and Archigram must have concluded that the only logical means of resisting was to fight to leave things pretty much alone.

But – happily and productively – Archigram had already deeply disturbed architecture, chipping away at its sense of discontinuity, eliding it with fields of objects and dreams. For Archigram, there was no need for all those received tensions between consumption and self-determination, between malleability and stability, between expendability and conservation, between high culture and low, and between freaks and swells. The proof was in the drawing. And, for a generation (mine), those drawings changed everything.

Michael Sorkin

Peter Cook's Archigram Entr'Acte – 1
THE BEGINNING

The discovery of the Warren Chalk, Dennis Crompton and Ron Herron group by the Peter Cook, David Greene and Mike Webb group was both simple and classic. The former three, as the core of various lists of names who with impressive regularity were given second prizes or 'mentions' in competitions and therefore published in the *Architect's Journal*, seemed mysterious and enviable from the perspective of the latter three. On sniffing-around, we were told that the prize-winners were all working at the London County Council – intellectually, the most recognised hotbed of the time (around 1961). After all, the Smithsons, Colin Rowe and pre-war

The members of the Archigram Group photographed in 1963 at the time of the Living City exhibition

Warren CHALK 1927–87
Born: London
Educated: Manchester College of Art

Peter COOK 1936–
Born: Southend on Sea
Educated: Bournemouth School of Art and the Architectural Association

Dennis CROMPTON 1935–
Born: Blackpool
Educated: Manchester University School of Architecture

modernists like Colin Lucas were there. We ploughed back some prize-money from the Gas House competition into *Archigram* 2, because we wanted this to be made up of *pages* … not just a broad sheet … and to have *invited* contributors – so why not ask these guys at the LCC?

Typically, Ron Herron was very friendly on the phone: 'Of course, why not?' So this first communication was very dry and direct. Cedric Price, who had a basement office across the street from James Cubitt's office (where David Greene and I worked) was, in a way, easier – yet Price was already somehow 'grand' and mysterious. Once Herron and the others met, it was very easy. David, Mike and I were very much 'just out of school' and *Archigram* – the pamphlet – a recalling of the enthusiasms of our respective

David GREENE 1937–
Born: Nottingham
Educated: Nottingham University School of Architecture

Ron HERRON 1930–94
Born: London
Educated: Brixton School of Building and Regent Street Polytechnic

Michael WEBB 1937–
Born: Henley on Thames
Educated: Regent Street Polytechnic

hothouses: Buckminster Fuller (at Greene's Nottingham), Stirling (who tutored Webb) and the Smithsons and Arthur Korn (who taught me at the AA).

Stumbling upon a Dada show in Dusseldorf in 1958 was enough for me, whereas Chalk and Herron had been party to conversations with the *actual* participants of the 'This is Tomorrow' exhibition. Heady stuff.

In the end this mixture of 'real build' (the other group had recently completed the South Bank complex) and seniority of contact didn't matter. Mike and I just got on with it and *drew*, whereas David was reading the beat poets: we were immersed in tensegrity masts, the *Evergreen Review* and Ornette Coleman.

Logo, Peter Taylor 1963

Theo Crosby's lead into the Institute of Contemporary Arts and some Gulbenkian money (I think £500, which I suppose is more like £15,000 now) set us all off on the exhibition project 'Living City'. With two friends – Peter Taylor (typographer) and Ben Fether (industrial designer) – we set about the task quite calmly, with twice-weekly meetings of the eight people (the six architects, of course, already working together at the Euston Station office of Taylor Woodrow with Crosby as both 'boss' and contact). His artist friends Eduardo Paolozzi and Joe Tilson became friends. When eventually shown, the Living City 'thing' ... the triangulated grotto of 'gloops' and statements that, through their demolition of formalised city concepts, exposed its love of the city – was compared (inevitably) with 'This is Tomorrow'.

Living City exhibition, whole group 1963

Certain similarities must have existed: we were too fond of Paolozzi to fly in his face; we were on the same side, after all. We didn't include any artists (as such) in our midst, but we more or less regarded ourselves as artists. A more intriguing set of comparisons

might revolve around the issue of *dynamic* and role-playing. An observation of the very different characteristics of Crosby, Hamilton, Paolozzi, the Smithsons, Stirling, Sandy Wilson, Frank Newby and Reyner Banham suggests that the power of 'This Is Tomorrow', in historical terms, was that of a type of 'blast-off'. The 'eager beaver' attributes of Crosby, the intellectual purity of Alison Smithson, the streetwise 'scholarship' of Hamilton – plus stories of Cedric Price as a rather fringe participant, sweeping the floor, so they say – had a certain recognition. The time gap between 'This Is Tomorrow' and 'Living City' was seven years, by the way.

For us, Dennis Crompton emerged rapidly as the person who could get us to do the thing – that is, actually *make* it; he taught Ron, Warren and me to weld (we constructed the frames in a shed at Euston). We learned about rubber grommets and clips, washers and timing switches from Dennis, typography from Peter Taylor, and about rubber edges from Ben. The intellectual necessity for that mixture of doubt and poetry was supplied by Warren and David. My own tendency to 'bustle about', I recognise, anyway – and Mike? Well, Mike is just a genius … that's about it!

Archigram Group in 1987

David GREENE   Warren CHALK   Peter COOK   Michael WEBB   Ron HERRON   Dennis CROMPTON

Archigram Classic
FURNITURE MANUFACTURERS ASSOCIATION HEADQUARTERS
Michael Webb, 1958

This project was designed in 1987–8 at the Regent Street Polytechnic as part of the fourth-year work. As a prestige building programme the designer was allowed considerable licence.

Planning

The building can be divided into three parts: the block of main accommodation, the vertical

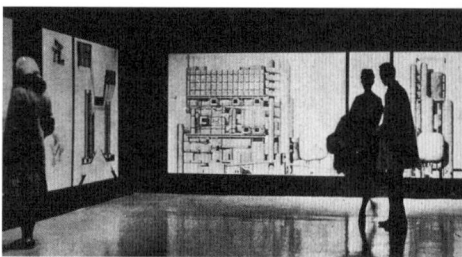
The projected exhibited at MOMA in New York in the early 60s

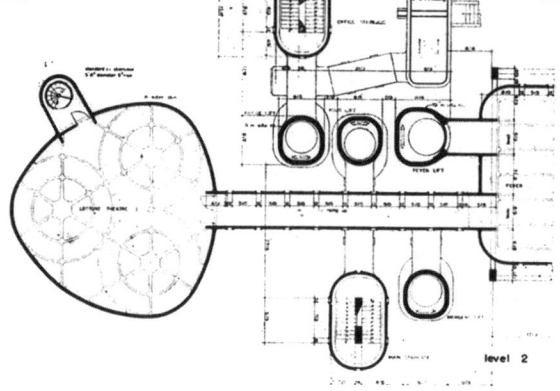

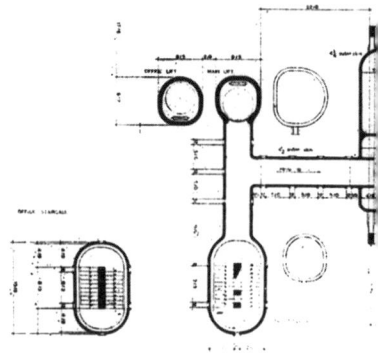

Furniture Factory

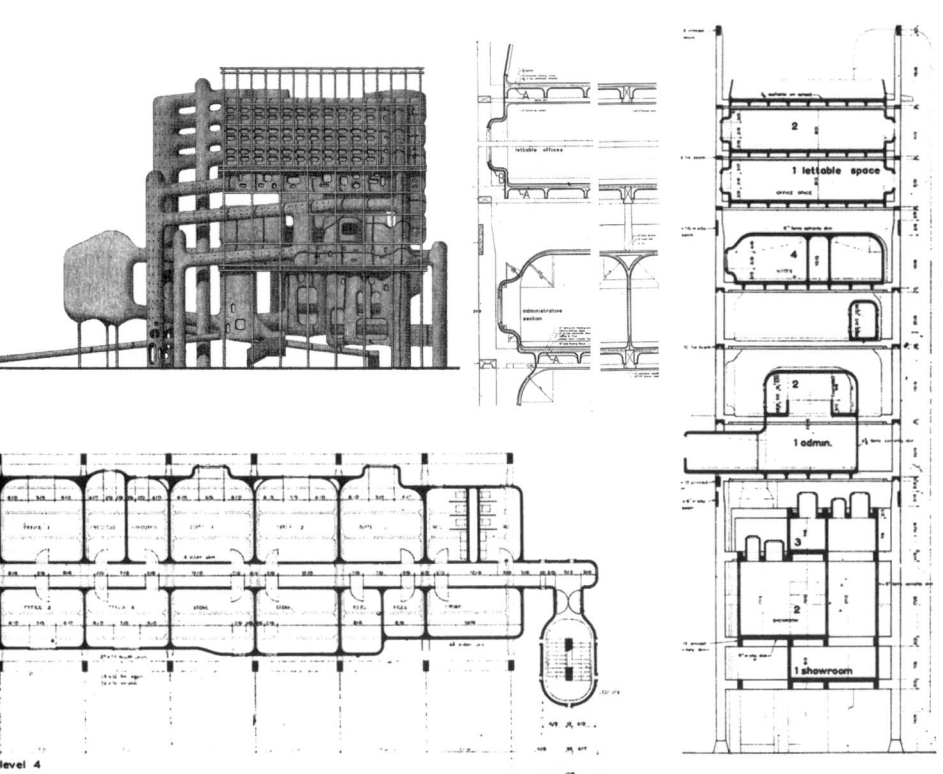

level 4

Michael Webb

circulation tubes, and the auditorium. The clubrooms, showrooms and offices for the FMA are situated on the lower floors of the main block. Above these are two floors of lettable offices. At either end are the clusters of vertical circulation. The auditorium is poised on the main axis above the entrance ramp.

Structure

Space enclosure is effected by means of pre-cast and in-situ Ferro-Cimento (a technique pioneered by Luigi Nervi, whereby various types of concrete are applied to layers of steel mesh). All the vertical parts of the fabric are of double skin construction. The outer, waterproof, membrane is 1 1/2 inches thick and the inner one is 4 inches of heat insulating vermiculite concrete. On the roof sections the outer layer is thickened. The concrete is applied by trowel and spray-gun to the mesh of reinforcement.

Research into site management and erection showed that it would be most economical to use pre-cast Ferro-Cimento floor trays. However, even with the rigidity that was gained by the use of curved forms, it was considered necessary to construct a supplementary frame. This frame, of pre-cast concrete, supports the floor trays at each level and facilitates easy erection.

Furniture Factory

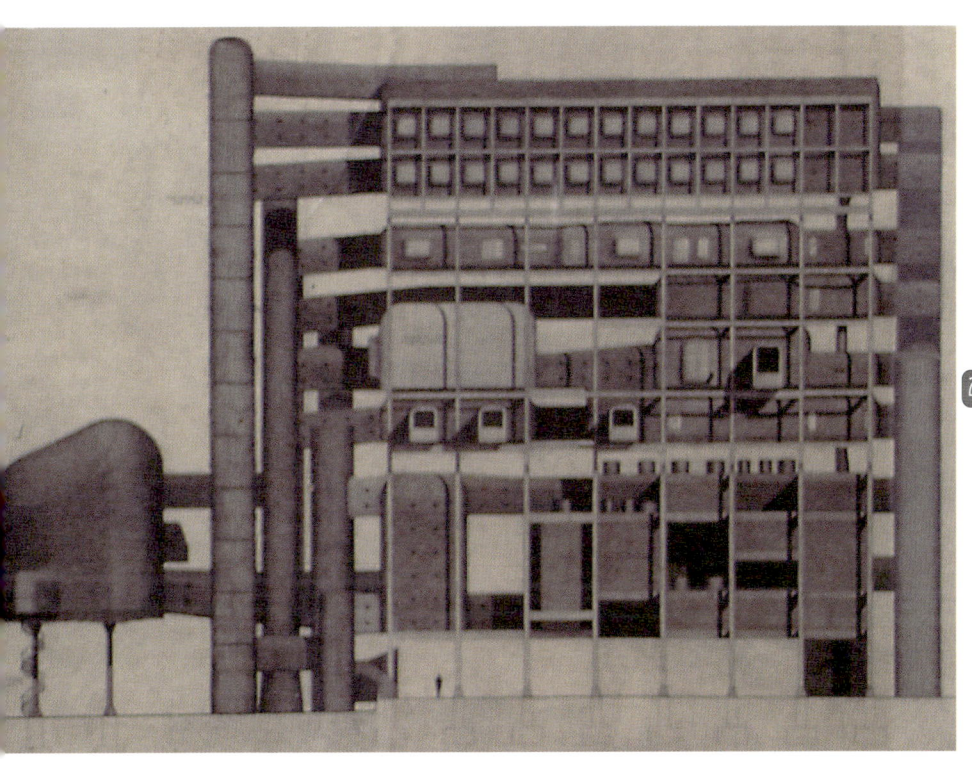

Michael Webb

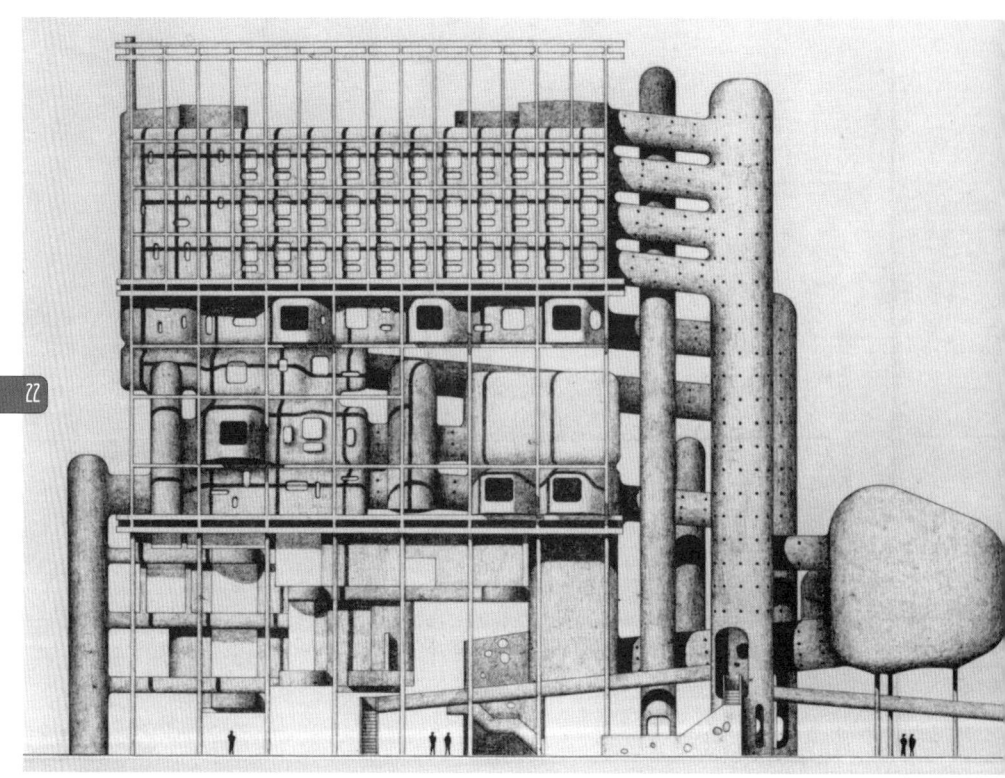

Furniture Factory

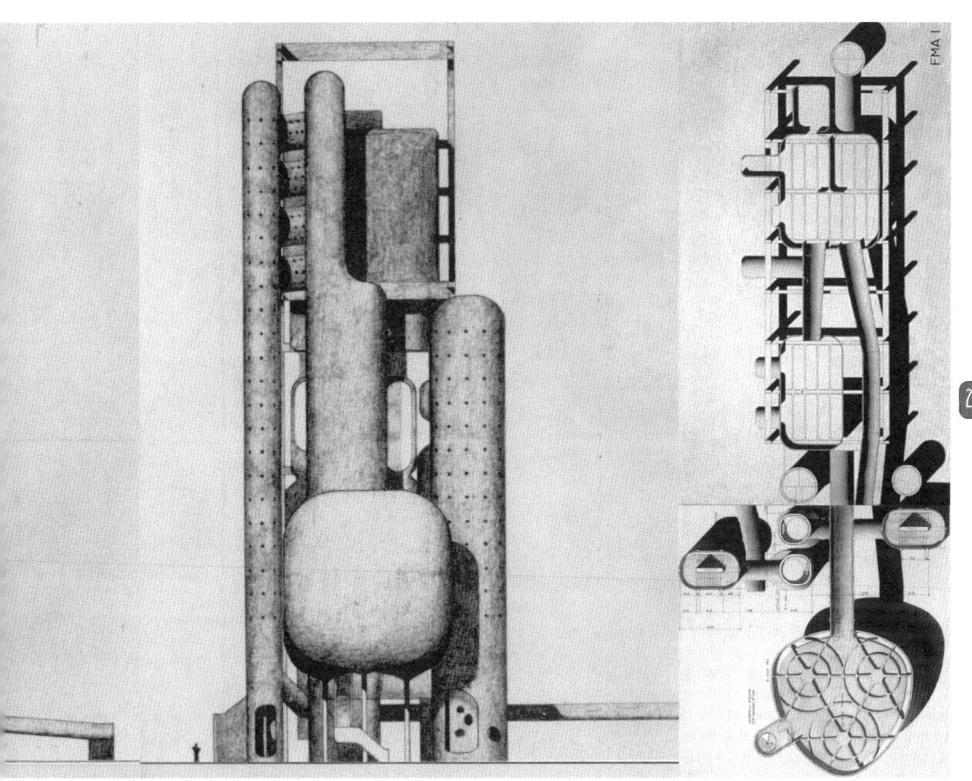

Michael Webb

Aesthetic and Execution

Mike Webb warned others of the formalistic trap that he fell into. He said at the time about his building;

At the sketch stage I adopted this form for the building before the exact technique by which it was to be made had been decided upon. Thus it was conceived primarily from an aesthetic point of view without any definite structural idea. In this lies the basic fault of the building and although the effect of taking the design through to the working-drawing stage has altered its appearance almost beyond recognition, it still retains much of the original artiness.

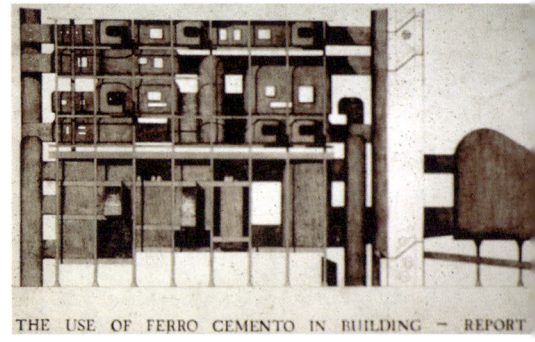

THE USE OF FERRO CEMENTO IN BUILDING — REPORT

When considering the economics of this building it should be remembered that with Ferro-Cimento a great saving is brought about by the lack of form-work (an item which accounts for up to 40 per cent of the cost in orthodox concrete work). Furthermore such components as the metal window and door frames are easily screwed onto the mesh reinforcement before concreting.

I am sure that such a building technique could be practical given some serious research. Nervi has shown us its potentialities in such buildings as the Gatti Wool Factory and the Turin Exhibition Hall. It now remains for us to continue his work.'

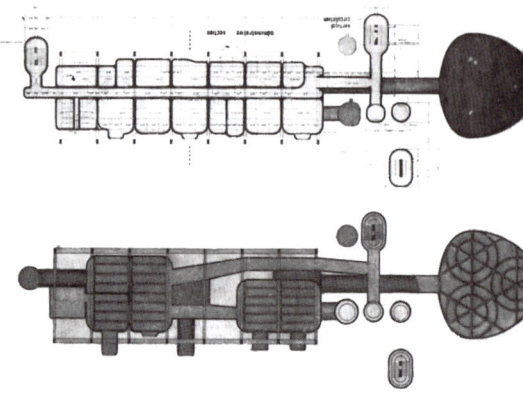

Furniture Factory

ARCHIGRAM – 'A Necessary Irritant'

Barry Curtis

The Progressive Intoxication of Modernism: British Architecture After 1945

In 1945 there was every indication that the immense rebuilding tasks presented to architects and planners by the devastation and neglect of wartime would be carried out according to modernist principles. Modernism was generally conceived as the appropriate style for a new social democratic settlement. It was a way of building which benefited from an accumulation of moral and functional concerns and integrated the experience of new methods and materials gained from the tactical necessities of total war. Modernism was ideologically opposed to the 'Völkisch' and to the undemocratic neo-classical grandeurs of totalitarianism. It was thought to be particularly appropriate to the democratic reasonableness which had inspired and sustained the war effort, offering a new relation to space and light and a sweeping away of signs of status and sentimentality.

The meaning of modern architecture was over-determined by notions of participation, equality and access; it was a style and a morality suitable for the 'sunlit uplands' of a new Britain. Modernism suggested an openness to the gaze, a metaphorically moral 'looking' which revealed structure and re-positioned the citizen at the centre of things. It offered a new rapport with nature and with the 'good' past. The rightness of modernism was invoked in numerous books, exhibitions and broadcasts which located themselves in a line of succession from the pioneering texts of the 1920s and 1930s. An affiliation to the modern implied a willingness to renounce comforts which were not primarily ergonomic or rational.

Unless otherwise indicated, quotes by Dennis Crompton (DC), Peter Cook (PC) and Ron Herron (RH) are from interviews with Barry Curtis and Philip Mann, February/March 1992. Mike Webb's comments are from an interview with Herbert Lachmeyer and Pascal Schöning, December 1991.

Barry Curtis

'Mies', Gropius and especially 'Corb' became the inspirational 'formgivers'; their work was interpreted and installed as ideal practice in architectural schools. Seminal modernist buildings were known to most students by their monochrome, strongly lit and uninhabited photographs. In the immediate post-war period opportunities to travel were very limited – Ron Herron was surprised, when he did visit France, to find that Le Corbusier's buildings were coloured. Accompanying deference to the 'Masters', there was a sense that modern architecture should take national and even local considerations into account. The British context could, to an extent, be domesticated and nationalised with reference to Georgian architecture and the Victorian engineering tradition. It could serve a continued interest in British vernaculars pioneered by the arts and crafts movement and the 'English Free School', detoured through the non-combatant, socially democratic Scandinavian countries which were deemed to have avoided the disruptions of revivalism, eclecticism and the aesthetic lapses which had vitiated British architecture. Modernism could indicate too, ways in which new forms could develop independently of the distasteful, modernistic futures formulated on the other side of the Atlantic.

Adjustments were required on the part of the post-war architectural profession. The 'People's War' and the coming to power of the Labour Party in 1945 suggested a need for architects who could combine the responsibilities of 'formgiving' with an ability to co-operate on complex, socially engineered planning schemes. The manifestoes of heroic modernism gave way to more explanatory, and on occasions, patronising addresses to the new citizen, delivered in a discursive form pioneered in wartime as 'information'. After the war, architects were more likely to be working for local planning authorities. The number of registered architects increased threefold in the twenty years after 1945, and a large percentage were in public employment. They were expected to invest more concern in sociological issues and to have a better understanding of new materials and building techniques.

John Summerson, writing in 1941 – a dangerous time for isolated and embattled Britain – foresaw a future, after the conclusion of hostilities, when architecture would no longer bear the responsibility of providing a 'symbolic cohesion' for society. He speculated that culture would be 'laid on like the water supply' and universal education would shape and structure public life. Architecture, he predicted, would be consigned to a servicing role. Summerson suggested that the 'Functionalist Crisis' which started with the translation of Corbusier's *Vers une Architecture* in 1927 would last for a generation and that 1957 would see 'a wider more adventurous conception' of architecture.[1]

1 John Summerson: 'The Mischievous Analogy', paper given at the Architectural Association in 1941, published as 'Essay IX' in *Heavenly Mansions* (Norton, New York 1963).

After the war there was a consensual feeling that architecture was a complex, socially ramified activity and that new technologies and social forces would play a part in activating the built environment. It became more difficult to consider architecture as a discrete matter between architect and client at a time of fundamental change. Reconstruction and planning were profoundly charged metaphors at a time when nationalisation, decolonisation and the installation of the welfare state were the work in hand. The narrowness and niceties of professional practice were critically rejected by a new generation of architects, many of whom had been students in the radical contexts of the 1930s. Trevor Dannant, surveying the contemporary architectural scene in 1959, seized on 1957 as a crucial watershed (and specifically January of that year, when the **M**[odern] **A**[rchitectural] **RS**[Research] Group was dissolved) – a moment, he suggested, when the 'intellectual' architects weaned on

Barry Curtis

Vers une Architecture gave way to 'an angrier generation'.[2]

In 1947 an article in *Architectural Design* magazine which captured the mood of the time, suggested necessary adjustments to any lingering individualism: 'we have to develop an aesthetic that is worthy of the good foundation already prepared in the studies of functionalism, sociology and science. There must be no relapse into wayward aestheticism … architecture is not one man thick.'[3] This statement suggests the extent to which architectural practice after the war was conceived as continuous with other social and scientific discourses. In many ways the debates on architecture which took place in the 1960s, in which Archigram played a prominent part, carried this assumption further to the point of dissolving architecture into a hybrid activity, or relinquishing it entirely to the needs of the client/consumer. Terms like 'psychotect' and 'psychosigner' were coined to indicate the extent to which new technologies and new social needs demanded the reformulation of socio-scientific professional practice. An editorial in the last *Architectural Design* of 1947 – a time of desperate hardship, rationing and shortage of building materials – looked forward to the long-awaited renaissance: 'For nearly fifteen years England has suffered under the shadow of war, from war itself and the aftermath of war. Before that for one hundred years she suffered the debasement of taste that accompanies an excess of too easily acquired wealth'.

Many of the books concerned with architecture and planning published in those fifteen years stress this debasement, a loss of proportion and functional simplicity parallelIng the moral lapse into laissez-faire capitalism, aggressive imperialism and moral hypocrisy. One solution was sought in the construction of an ideal Georgian style which was heavily over-determined. 'Georgian' could speak to

2 Trevor Dannant: *Modern Architecture in Britain* (Batsford, London 1959).

3 Mark Hartland Thomas: *Architectural Design*, January 1947.

'A Necessary Irritant'

the need for aristocratic taste, organic community, decorative propriety, or domesticated classicism. Of particular significance after the experience of a highly technological war effort was the sense of a civilised architectural style based on unitary construction; a redeeming modular rationale which paralleled, at the domestic level, the mechanical genius of the early industrial revolution.

In the work of writers like Pevsner, Giedion, Summerson, Fry, Read, Tubbs, Brett, Robertson, Williams-Ellis, Sharp, Richards and Gloag there is a remarkable consistency of aesthetic, functional and moral judgement. Their writings make fundamental assumptions regarding the evolving modernist project in post-war Britain. They suggest the need to adapt to traditional values, to humanise and mature the uncompromising style of the heroic inter-war years. Their aim was to balance the grand, international narrative of modernism against a revisionary Britishness. In 1945 there was a renewed interest in national identity; the neo-romanticism of the 1930s and the heightened iconography of the war years were drawn on to construct a new visual identity for a nation now isolated from its Empire and tentatively closer to Europe. Britain was represented in the Festival of 1951 as a country rediscovering its 'land', reformulating its history and reconceiving its future. Archigram inherited some of the revisionary anticipation of a technologically rich future, whilst at the same time trailing clouds of the eccentric inventive spirit which the Festival celebrated in its 'Lion and Unicorn' pavilion.

In 1951, the Festival of Britain provided a model for the integration of new technologies with a new image and mode of address for architecture. The citizens of a technologically rational, post-imperial and increasingly post-industrial Britain were invited to adopt a picturesque, allusive and celebratory relationship to the past as a

Barry Curtis

conscious 'post-modernism'. Pleasure became an important issue, specifically in relation to the Festival but more generally as part of the imperative to adapt the austerities of modernism to the requirements of everyday life. Light, space and proportion were intended to produce a new order of pleasurable response. The aristocratic spaces of park and square were to be brought into a new relationship with the demotic entertainments of the seaside, the fairground and pleasure garden. Howard Robertson in 1944 referred architects to Blackpool as a model, a 'dream of paradise'.[4] Clough Williams-Ellis, for whom pleasure was a central concern, suggested that the grotesque scenarios of 'Monk' Lewis and the technological whimsy of Heath Robinson provided specifically national formats for environments of pleasure. Nationalised modernism was to provide a structure around which the decorative and evocative could flourish.

Blackpool in the 1990s

4 Howard Robertson: *Architecture Arising* (Faber, London 1944).

The British, in particular, were conceived as having a picturesque sensibility with strong resistance to an ordered aesthetic and a regimented life. British vernacular was thought to be particularly affiliated to crowded, and sentimentally invested, mises en scène. The Festival mobilised this aesthetic, drawing on the topographic potential of modernist styles of building and planning. Battersea Gardens provided scope for an intensive exploration of theatrical and whimsical effects. The fantasies of Roland Emmett, who designed the much-visited and celebrated 'Oyster Creek and Far Tottering Railway', as well as the imagery of antique cars, canal boats and hot-air balloons, represented an acceptable form of the surreal whimsy that modernism repressed. In a discussion recorded

'A Necessary Irritant'

in *Ark* 42 (1968), Warren Chalk and Cedric Price respectively rejected the two poles between which Archigram sought to operate – 'a ridiculous Emmett level ' and 'dreary Bauhaus logic'.

It is in these post-war shifts in architectural values – the sense of an architecture responsive to social need, more efficient, more pleasurable, in touch with new technologies, modularised and capable of servicing everyday wants – that some of the themes that were to emerge in the work of Archigram only fifteen years after the end of the war can be discerned. There are glimpses of a 'high-tech' future in the massive engineering projects of wartime – the Thames forts on which Ron Herron's father was a gunner, the Mulberry Harbours and the new technologies of aircraft engineering, which the young Reyner Banham was delighted to see applied to buildings in the Festival of Britain. As Dennis Crompton has said: 'Barnes Wallis [the inventor of the Bouncing Bomb among other things] could only be British.' Less dramatic but more pervasive were the attempts to bring prefabricated housing into the civilian realm. John Madge, in the introduction to *Tomorrow's Houses*,[5] attempted to summarise the technical advances in house building made possible by the war and to bring 'the hard light of reality to bear on a field which for too long has remained a copywriters' paradise.' This pragmatic tone was kept alive in the avant-garde manifestoes of the 1950s and 1960s, which attempted to bring together both sides of the equation – to provide basic services whilst acknowledging the importance of the aspirations and fantasies that were stimulated and realised by the expanding culture of consumerism.

For a new generation of post-war architects, recipients of education

The Thames forts

5 John Madge: *Tomorrow's Houses* (Pilot Press, London 1946).

Barry Curtis

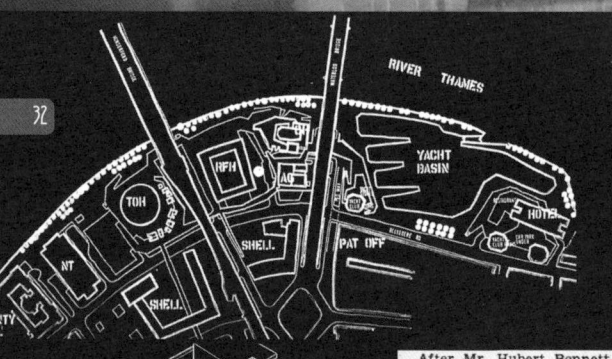

After Mr. Hubert Bennett, architect to the Council, had explained to them, his team of assistants, intelligent enthusiastic young men in crew cuts and Italian suits, listened anxiously to the comments.

One of them explained. "We would like to see flats and cinemas on the South Bank too, so that it becomes alive; a place where people live and enjoy themselves in different ways, rather than just a cultural centre."

South Bank Development, LCC 1960-62

'A Necessary Irritant'

Plug-in Paddington East, Peter Cook 1966

6 Warren Chalk, Ark 42, 1968.

Tuning London's South Bank, Ron Herron 1972

grants and beneficiaries of a massive increase in public-sector employment, the politics and visionary modernism of the 'generation of 1936' and the awesome achievements of wartime continued to be an influence. Ron Herron, Warren Chalk and Dennis Crompton worked on London's South Bank site and combined the aesthetics of post-war Le Corbusier with the form and finish of military installations. The South Bank's monumental, bunker aesthetic belongs very much to New Brutalism, but its multi-dimensional planning and conspicuous services generate a silhouette which prefigures the plug-in aesthetic of Archigram's later projects. Perhaps most importantly, the South Bank site remains a rare example of three-dimensional architecture and continues to function in the permissive way which was to become part of the Archigram morality and aesthetic. Sadly, the structure, 'where people will just assemble the bits and pieces that they collect together themselves'[6] has become a shelter for the nomads of the 1990s, a sign of independence without the technological enhancement which Archigram sought for the citizens of the future.

A new toughness and the interest in commercial vernacular that emerged in opposition to the new-empirical, picturesque and historicist reformulations of modernism were evident in the uneasy grouping of work which came to be known as New Brutalism. Reyner Banham, in his commentary on that tendency,[7] saw it as an international phenomenon with complex origins and affiliations. It was conceived as an aesthetic allied to the paintings and sculptures of art brut and also, in part, to the regulations and symmetries of the new Palladianism. Its structures and textures were indebted to the later work of Le Corbusier as well as to the wartime 'architecture of aggression'. One of its distinguishing characteristics was a new kind of sociological interest in the 'real life of cities' and in the possibility of providing a complete environment. This aspiration was underwritten by a sense of the importance of understanding how people lived and what they wanted in addition to what they needed.

The penetration of sociological texts into the culture of the 1950s is evident in the 'kitchen-sink' aesthetic of closely observed detail in painting, literature and film. A key text was Richard Hoggart's chapter entitled 'Landscape with Figures', a testimony to the integrities of a disappearing working-class culture in his influential book *The Uses of Literacy*.[8] An interest in the details of street life, as described by Willmott and Young in the East End of London[9] and in the Opie's investigations of children's games,[10] is evident too in Nigel Henderson's photographs of Bethnal Green, taken at a time when his wife, an anthropologist, was working for Mass Observation, in the early 1950s. The photographs were subsequently used by Alison and Peter Smithson to illustrate their text *Urban Structuring*.[11] Archigram developed a practice of montaging photographs onto drawn elevations which had been used extensively by the Smithsons in the early 1950s. Street life was regarded as a given for the Smithsons, to be incorporated into new structures which would respect the realm of 'passing presence' and 'chance encounter'.

7 Reyner Banham: *The New Brutalism: Ethic or Aesthetic?* (Architectural Press, London 1966).

8 Richard Hoggart: *The Uses of Literacy* (Chatto & Windus, London 1957).
9 Peter Willmott and Michael Young: *Family and Kinship in East London* (Routledge & Kegan Paul, London 1966).
10 Iona and Peter Opie: *The Lore and Language of Schoolchildren* (Oxford University Press 1959).
11 Alison and Peter Smithson: *Urban Structuring* (Studio Vista, London 1967).

'A Necessary Irritant'

Tuned Suburb, Ron Herron 1968

Oasis, Ron Herron 1968

12 Robert Venturi, Denise Scott Brown and Steven Izenour: *Learning from Las Vegas* (MIT Press, Cambridge, Mass. 1972).

Barry Curtis

In Archigram's late 1960s' montages of 'Tuned Suburbs' and 'Oasis', the adults are at play among a more deconstructed urban landscape. These themes, which are continuous from the work of the brutalists to Archigram, testify to the extent to which the architects regarded themselves as complicit with the future inhabitants of their projects – a sensibility significantly lacking in the town-planning texts they were reacting against. The principle of acceptance, of the 'artist as consumer', was pioneered by the theorists and practitioners of the Independent Group and aphoristically elevated by Robert Venturi in the 1960s to the principle that 'Main Street is nearly right.'[12] A sense of the existential immediacy of the city is an important component of the architectural radicalism of the 1950s – Ian Nairn expressed something of the spirit of the new sociologically conscious urbanism and its reaction against the morality of welfarism, calling in 1959 for 'a city for tarts as well as good girls, for spivs as well as model husbands'.[13]

The official orthodoxies of town planning and urban renewal were far removed from this spirit of sympathetic anthropological involvement. Wilfred Burns, author of the influential *New Towns for Old*,[14] was dedicated to simplifying the: 'early nineteenth-century muddle of congested housing and factories' of London. He argued that the devastating effect of slum clearance on: 'social groupings built up over the years' could be described as 'a good thing when we are dealing with people who have no initiative or civic pride', adding vindictively: 'though the people seem to be satisfied with their miserable environment and seem to enjoy an extrovert social life in their own locality'. Archigram never mentioned any uprootings which would be necessary for the inhabitants of their own projects but seemed to assume, in the spirit of the radical architecture of the time, that the move would be motivated by the attraction of an active involvement in the pursuit of pleasure and mobility.

One of the characteristics of brutalism was termed by the Smithsons 'the topological mode' (used particularly to describe their scheme for Sheffield University and later employed to describe their proposals for the Park Hill estate in Sheffield). This interest in three-dimensional planning is evident in the early work of Ron Herron, Warren Chalk and Dennis Crompton on the South Bank, and is fundamental to the schemes of Archigram. The brutalist ethos, combining in characteristic avant-garde fashion a synthesis of the 'primitive' and the futuristic, involved a de-territorialising of the modernist conventions of the time. This

13 Ian Nairn: Encounter 65, vol.12, February 1959, quoted in Bryan Appleyard: *The Pleasures of Peace* (Faber, London 1989).

14 Wilfred Burns: *New Towns for Old: The Technique of Urban Renewal* (Leonard Hill, London 1963).

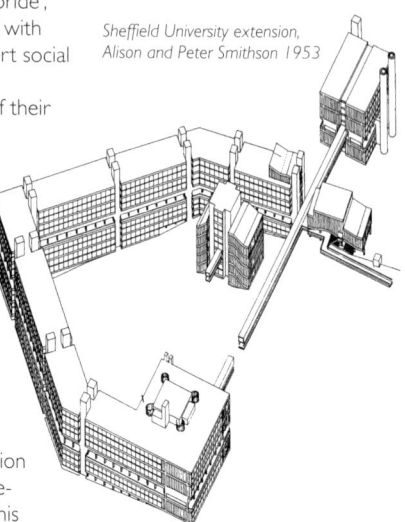

Sheffield University extension, Alison and Peter Smithson 1953

'A Necessary Irritant'

combination was very much in evidence at the 'This is Tomorrow' exhibition, held at the Whitechapel Gallery, London, in 1956, which featured celebrations of the most modern and forward-looking forms of mass-produced entertainment, and vernacular, junkyard-brut with a suggestion of nuclear devastation.

The Smithsons were interested in the basic characteristics of architecture, a new fundamentalism which drew on the sensuous and standardised forms of Japanese architecture and re-explored Le Corbusier's interest in vernaculars through regionally specific work like Candilis's Moroccan housing projects. The emphasis of this new attention to the textures of living was visited on: 'architecture as the direct result of a way of life'. The logic of this approach suggested a radical re-evaluation of architecture for a clientele immersed in the activities dictated by consumer capitalism but willing to regard themselves, at the same time, as 'primitives of a new sensibility', affiliated to the Ur-texts of design. The work of Archigram frequently followed and developed the frisson of figuratively juxtaposing the astronaut and the atavist. A similar conjuncture was exploited by Terence Conran in the combination of 'primitive' and modern goods on sale in his first Habitat shop in May 1964. In some respects this was a familiar dialectic of modernism, a strategy for exploring the 'others' of bourgeois, passé-ist culture, but for Archigram it took on a novel dimension in their stress on the dematerialising potential of new technologies and software. This electronic empowerment, they predicted, would lead to a new nomadic relation to nature. Archigram modified the futurist project of early modernism to a distinctly post-war sensibility which in the late 1950s began to engage with an awareness of cybernetics, software and ecological concerns.

Between the CIAM conference of 1951 and the Otterlo

Barry Curtis

conference of 1959 urbanism was a central concern for debate. In 1951, at Hoddesdon the non-professional contribution to the life of the city was acknowledged and discussed under the heading of 'Urban Spontaneity'. Oscar Newman, in his 'Short Review of CIAM Activity'[15] indicated the extent to which the concerns of 1950 were different from those of 1930. Twenty years and one devastating war on from the heroic formulations on tall buildings, collective life and general principles were not viable. The solutions sought in 1950 were more empirical, respectful of particular situations and employed techniques of renewal and extension.

It is difficult to establish the extent to which the dissemination of these ideas coincided with the accessing of sociological texts by younger British architects. It is also hard to establish how influential the work of the situationists may have been on Archigram. Ivan Chtcheglov, under the pseudonym Gilles Ivain, published in *International Situationiste 1* (1958) his 'Formula For a New City',[16] which incorporated many of the ideas of mobility and fun later developed in the work of Archigram. The work of the French Marxist Henri Lefebvre and his writings on 'everyday life' may have been influential on the thinking of some of the members of CIAM in the 1950s. Certainly, the work of Constant was well known to the members of Archigram via the journal *L'Architecture d'Aujourd'hui* and, more directly, as the result of a lecture in London – which impressed them with its daring but disappointed because of the lack of detailed specification.

At Otterlo in 1959 a controversial debate took place as the result of a detailed attack mounted by Peter Smithson on Ernesto Rogers' Milanese tower block, the Torre Velasca. Rogers was accused of embodying 'three kinds of short sightedness' – eclecticism, regionalism and historicism. Smithson addressed a perceived

15 Oscar Newman: CIAM '59 in *Otterlo: Documents of Modern Architecture* (Alec Tiranti, London 1961).

16 Ivan Chtcheglov: 'Formulary for a New Urbanism' (October 1953), collected in Ken Knaab (ed.): *Situationist International Anthology* (Bureau of Public Secrets, Berkeley, California, 1989).

'A Necessary Irritant'

NeoBabylone, Constant Niewenhuis 1962–63

17 Oscar Newman, op. cit.

absence of any qualities in the building which were 'exemplary or re-usable'.[17] Smithson's favoured criticism was spoken from a position which demanded a new modern vernacular. The dispute was part of a relativisation of architecture, a realisation of the provisional nature of architectural forms and conventions expressed in a more radical way at the International Dialogue on Experimental Architecture (IDEA) Conference, organised by Archigram at Folkestone in 1966, where the phrase: 'Architecture is only a cultural solution to the problem of enclosure' indicated their fundamentalist mood. More significantly for the later work of Archigram, the sense of architecture as relative and pragmatic speaks to the role of the architect in creating universally valid solutions with no necessary responsibility or respect for place. At the same time it signals a restoration of the heroic aspirations of the previous generation of modernists to provide an architecture coherent with the latest developments in technology and responsive to its capacity to create and service needs.

Barry Curtis

IT'S ALL THE SAME

THESE

'A Necessary Irritant'

It's All The Same: Precursors and Influences

The Independent Group, meeting at the Institute of Contemporary Arts in London from 1952, had posed a comprehensive challenge to the values embodied in the theory and practice of the architectural and design establishment. Reyner Banham offered a re-evaluation of modernism combining an enthusiasm for its radical values with a critique of its failure to grasp the principles of engineering and the potentialities of technology. Banham had been introduced to the work of Buckminster Fuller by John McHale and Fuller became the embodiment of the forces of technological transfer which he endorsed.

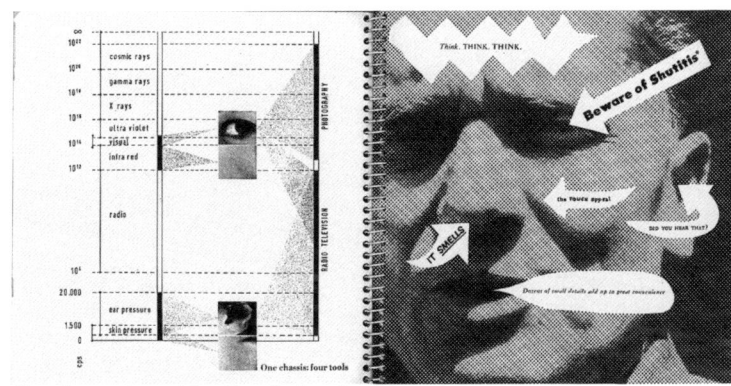

'This is Tomorrow' spread from Group Two's section of the catalogue

John Voelcker, a collaborator with Richard Hamilton and McHale on the influential 'Group Two' exhibit at 'This is Tomorrow', was one of the young architects who joined with the Smithsons' Team 10 in

Barry Curtis

challenging the orthodoxies of the Athens Charter and sought to introduce a new complexity which could respond to 'belonging' as a basic emotional need: 'From "belonging" – identity – comes the enriching sense of neighbourliness. The short narrow street of the slum succeeds where spacious redevelopment frequently fails.'[18] Richard Hamilton's interest in product design, advertising and marketing enabled him to oppose the principles of 'good design' in the interests of planned obsolescence and consumer engineering.

18 John McHale, in Newman, op. cit.

This cover of Living Arts 2 was arranged by Richard Hamilton and photographed by Robert Freeman. The catalogue for Archigram's Living City exhibition formed a section of the publication. 1963

'A Necessary Irritant'

Young intellectuals in other realms of cultural production shared with the Independent Group a strong sense of irreverence and a passionate autodidacticism. In writing, film making, painting and sculpture a similar mood was evident – a questioning of elitist values and a willingness to engage with the generic, banal, consumerist and technological sensibilities of a rapidly modernising culture.

Anthony Sampson, writing his ambitious overview of the state of the nation in the early 1960s, located the twin themes of tradition and innovation at the heart of a rapidly changing culture.[19] The impulses to modernise took many forms – including wider access to higher education and the imaginative pursuit of a more cosmopolitan, classless, multi-cultural Britain. The attack on cultural enclaves and vested interests paralleled Archigram's rejection of 'Architecture'. With the contention that 'Everything is the Same',[20] Archigram joined in the wider project of cultural levelling.

One of the intangible consequences of the vitalising democracy of wartime and the immediate post-war experience was a newly visible inventiveness and ingenuity – a collage sensibility which involved a refusal to recognise boundaries and respect hierarchies. Wartime vindicated the surreal imagination of the pre-war avant-garde; perverse logic and *reductio ad absurdum* entered into a productive symbiosis with the technological imagination. A strand of humour which can be traced from comedy shows such as 'It's That Man Again' via 'The Goon Show' and 'Beyond the Fringe' to 'Monty Python's Flying Circus' was dedicated to exploring the absurdity of normality, the surreality of ideas taken to their limits and the potential of inversions and logical substitutions. The imperatives of Archigram – the 'what if …' and 'this will upset them …' – suggest similar comic/satiric impulses in their work.

Certainly the British tradition of crackpot invention which occurred

19 Anthony Sampson: *Anatomy of Britain* (Hodder & Stoughton, London 1962).

20 Archigram 3, 1963.

Barry Curtis

at the intersection of radical logic and limited resources, was one source of inspiration for them. Archigram located themselves as inventors and as highly intelligent consumers searching for more satisfying goods, services and solutions. Richard Hamilton, in an essay written in 1961, points to a new symbiosis of the time: 'It is positive Dada, creative where Dada was destructive. Perhaps it is Mama – a cross fertilisation of Futurism and Dada which upholds a respect for the culture of the masses and a conviction that the artist in twentieth-century urban life is inevitably a consumer of mass culture and potentially a contributor to it.'[21]

21 Richard Hamilton: 'For the Finest Art, Try Pop' (*Gazette* 1, 1961), *Collected Words* (Thames & Hudson, London 1983).

The impact of Archigram was largely attributable to a combination of extraordinary visual complexity and a dedication to use and pleasure. With the Independent Group's recognition of the 'push-pin' culture, fostered by the post-war availability of abundant images, by the mid 1950s the juxtaposition and confrontation of ubiquitous pictures had become an inspirational condenser of meanings and an inspiration to creativity. Collage, which became an increasingly popular means of communication among artists and designers, implies an autodidactic and polysemic position from which the new configurations make sense – an expression of the enhanced authority of the consumer/artist. Archigram speaks eloquently to the new world of product-experiences. Banham once described the exhilarating perspective offered to young creators who were willing to submit to the empowering claims of consumer culture as 'a louche situation'.[22]

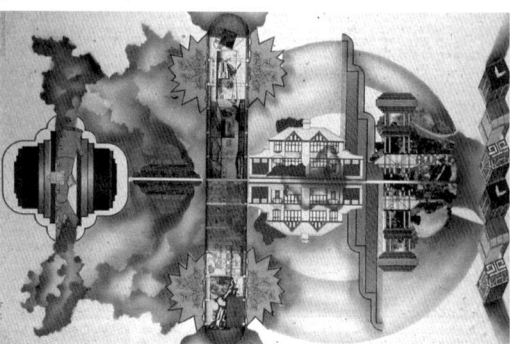

The Archigram Robot 1, Peter Cook 1973

22 Reyner Banham, title of lecture delivered at the ICA in 1973.

'A Necessary Irritant'

Clusters in the Air, Arata Isozaki, 1962

Structure for a Spacial Town, Yona Friedman, 1964

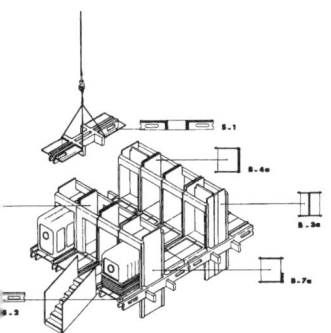
Assembly system for a prefabricated appartment building, Kisho Kurokawa, 1962

In order to re-establish links with the vitality of modernism, it was necessary for young architects to look beyond the British context, as well as beyond the conventional realms of architecture. One attractive direction was the rapidly proliferating area of product design and the landscape of popular consumption and use. The growth of the British economy in the late 1950s meant that the shock of the domestic 'new', first encountered ten years before by the Independent Group in the pages of American magazines, was beginning to figure in the material environment. In the direction of experimental architecture, Archigram corresponded with the Japanese Metabolists, Italian Urbanists – the Citta Territorio Group, Constant, Yona Friedman and other architects featured in journals like *L'Architecture d'Aujourd'hui*. Their contribution to this international discourse was a particular interest in detailed specification which, Reyner Banham suggested, owes something to the rigorous tradition of the British architectural school 'crit'. Unique among the experimentalists and utopians of the time,

Barry Curtis

Archigram produced drawings which were very specific. Dennis Crompton, commenting on the pragmatic blueprint nature of Archigram's visionary drawings, said of them, 'If they could draw them, I could build them.'

The Archigram project is remarkable in retrospect for its confidence and its simultaneous irreverence and seriousness. It shares with other projects conceived at that time an absolute conviction in the possibility of a more functional, more pleasurable future, and a sense of the arbitrariness of accepted values. In early issues of *Archigram*, contributors focused on two key issues: the false distinction between architecture and other consumable products, and the stubborn resistance of architects to the idea of impermanent structures. In *Archigram* 3, Peter Cook drew attention to the deceptions involved in making buildings appear to be dignified and irreplaceable objects. From these early projects the central aim of Archigram was to 'unmask' architecture and to demonstrate that the services and technology could speak for themselves.

It is difficult to place Archigram in relation to the architectural debates which were taking place in the early years of the careers of Ron Herron and Warren Chalk, before the other members of the group started their training. In one respect Archigram belonged to the new sensibility which sought to re-evaluate architectural practice and to redefine the nature of architecture itself. The individuals who came together to constitute the group in 1963 clearly shared an enthusiasm for the richness and contradictions of urban life and distanced themselves from the abstract solutions of authoritarian modernism. On the other hand, they showed little affiliation to the sociological interests of the slightly older generation represented by Team 10, as the Smithson/Voelcker group became known after 1956.

'A Necessary Irritant'

1 DISCUSSION

ON OTHER PAGES: 2 PROBLEM 3 GROUNDWORK 4 PROJECTS 5 ACCEPTANCE
FOLLOWED BY : 6 LIVING CITY IN RETROSPECT

ALMOST WITHOUT REALISING IT, WE HAVE ABSORBED INTO OUR LIVES THE FIRST GENERATION OF EXPENDABLES......FOODBAGS, PAPER TISSUES, POLYTHENE WRAPPERS, BALLPENS, E.P'S.... SO MANY THINGS ABOUT WHICH WE DON'T HAVE TO THINK. WE THROW THEM AWAY ALMOST AS SOON AS WE ACQUIRE THEM.

ALSO WITH US ARE THE ITEMS THAT ARE BIGGER AND LAST LONGER, BUT ARE NEVERTHELESS PLANNED FOR OBSOLESCENCE......THE MOTOR CAR......AND ITS UNIT-BUILT GARAGE.

NOW THE SECOND GENERATION IS UPON US - PAPER FURNITURE IS A REALITY IN THE 'STATES, PAPER SHEETS ARE A REALITY IN BRITISH HOSPITAL BEDS, THE LONDON COUNTY COUNCIL IS PUTTING UP LIMITED-LIFE-SPAN HOUSES.

THROUGH AND THROUGH

EVERY LEVEL OF SOCIETY AND WITH EVERY LEVEL OF COMMODITY, THE UNCHANGING SCENE IS BEING REPLACED BY THE INCREASE IN CHANGE OF OUR USER-HABITS - AND THEREBY, EVENTUALLY, OUR USER-HABITATS.

WE ARE BECOMING MUCH MORE USED TO THE IDEA OF CHANGING A PIECE OF CLOTHING YEAR-BY-YEAR, RATHER THAN EXPECT TO HANG ON TO IT FOR SEVERAL YEARS. SIMILARLY, THE IDEA OF KEEPING A PIECE OF FURNITURE LONG ENOUGH TO BE ABLE TO HAND IT ON TO OUR CHILDREN IS BECOMING INCREASINGLY RIDICULOUS.
IN THIS SITUATION, WE SHOULD NOT BE SURPRISED IF SUCH ARTICLES WEAR OUT WITHIN THEIR 'WELCOME-LIFE' SPAN, RATHER THAN THEIR TRADITIONAL LIFE-SPAN.

THE ATTITUDE OF MIND THAT ACCEPTS SUCH A SITUATION IS CREEPING INTO OUR SOCIETY AT ABOUT THE RATE THAT EXPENDABLE GOODS BECOME AVAILABLE. WE MUST RECOGNISE THIS AS A HEALTHY AND ALTOGETHER POSITIVE SIGN. IT IS THE PRODUCT OF A SOPHISTICATED CONSUMER SOCIETY, RATHER THAN A STAGNANT (AND IN THE END, DECLINING) SOCIETY.

OUR COLLECTIVE MENTAL BLOCKAGE OCCURS BETWEEN THE LAND OF THE SMALL-SCALE CONSUMER-PRODUCTS, AND THE OBJECTS WHICH MAKE UP OUR ENVIRONMENT. PERHAPS IT WILL NOT BE UNTIL SUCH THINGS AS HOUSING, AMENITY-PLACE AND WORKPLACE BECOME RECOGNISED AS CONSUMER PRODUCTS THAT CAN BE 'BOUGHT OFF THE PEG' - THAT ALL THIS IMPLIES IN TERMS OF EXPENDABILITY (FOREMOST), INDUSTRIALISATION, UP-TO-DATE-NESS, CONSUMER-CHOICE, AND BASIC PRODUCT-DESIGN - THAT WE CAN BEGIN TO MAKE AN ENVIRONMENT THAT IS REALLY PART OF A DEVELOPING HUMAN CULTURE.

WHY IS THERE AN INDEFINABLE RESISTANCE TO PLANNED OBSOLESCENCE FOR A KITCHEN, WHICH IN TWELVE YEARS WILL BE HIGHLY INEFFICIENT (BY THE STANDARDS OF THE DAY) AND IN TWENTY YEARS WILL BE INTOLERABLE, YET THERE ARE NO QUALMS ABOUT FOUR YEARS OBSOLESCENCE FOR CARS.

THE IDEA OF AN EXPENDABLE ENVIRONMENT IS STILL SOMEHOW REGARDED AS AKIN TO ANARCHY.... AS IF, IN ORDER TO MAKE IT WORK, WE WOULD BULLDOZE WESTMINSTER ABBEY.

WE SHALL NOT BULLDOZE WESTMINSTER ABBEY

ADDED TO THIS, THE IDEA OF A NON-PERMANENT BUILDING HAS OVERTONES OF ECONOMY, AUSTERITY, BUILT REFLECTION OF THE SECOND HALF OF THE TWENTIETH CENTURY. MOST OF THE BUILDINGS THAT EXIST THAT ARE TECHNICALLY EXPENDABLE, HAVE THE FACT SKILFULLY HIDDEN.....THEY MASQUERADE AS PERMANENT BUILDINGS - MONUMENTS TO THE PAST.

ON THE VISUAL PAGES WE SHOW (2) THE SELL-OUT TO THE PAST OF OUR PRESENT SHOWING OF 'POP' EXPENDABLE BUILDINGS.....BUT AGAINST THE REAL ATTEMPTS TO DO SOMETHING MORE......BY (3) FEATURES THE BASIC COMPONENT AND FORMAL INVESTIGATIONS THAT ARE FORMING THE EARLY HISTORICAL PERIOD FOR EXPENDABILITY.
(4) IS A COLLECTION OF PROJECTS WHICH BEGIN TO EXTEND THE RANGE OF EXPENDABLE ARCHITECTURE (5) THE SINGLE CELL IN THE SINGLE SITUATION.....THAT THE HOME, THE WHOLE CITY, AND THE (6) ATTEMPTS A SUMMING-UP WITH OUR BASIC MESSAGE.
FROZEN PEA PACK ARE ALL THE SAME.....

Editorial page from Archigram 3

In retrospect, Archigram seem to have identified more closely with some of the enthusiasms and manifestoes of the Independent Group and in many respects to have endorsed the user-led aesthetic of Hamilton and the revisionary modernism of Banham, both of whom were well known to the group socially. It is always difficult to register the slight shifts in sensibility which seem to define the shadow line between generational concerns, but the early 1960s produced a comprehensive revision of the ideological and visual register comprising new attitudes to 'subjective realism', a shift from 'seriousness' to 'fun' and into an imaginative realm where it was possible to make radical disjunctures between ideas and attitudes which had previously seemed contingent and symbiotic. Archigram found it possible to restore the heroic momentum of modernism, to 'take their desires for reality' and to 'demand the impossible'[23] with the technologically sustained reasonableness of the time.

The relationship of Archigram to the members of the Independent Group was a close and sociable one. Reyner Banham overlooked, advised and propagated the work of the young architects. He was the critic and historian most concerned with revealing the extent to which architecture is as much about mechanical services as it is about structure. Banham's *Guide to Modern Architecture*,[24] seeks to admit engineers into the canon of great modern architects, mentioning Nervi, Torroja, Catalano, Candela, Fuller, Defaille and Otto. He celebrates the conformities between their work and the disposable culture of the new domestic landscape, referring to Fuller's dome for the Tenth Milan Triennale as 'like making up the models on the back of cereal packets', and he describes Ionel Schein as 'the newest hero of the mass-production dream'.

In 1969, in *The Architecture of the Well-Tempered Environment*,[25]

23 Graffiti photographed in Paris, May 1968, in Christopher Gray (ed. and translator): *Leaving the Twentieth Century* (Free Fall Publications, London 1974).

24 Reyner Banham: *Guide to Modern Architecture* (Architectural Press, London 1962).

25 Reyner Banham: *The Architecture of the Well-Tempered Environment* (Architectural Press, 1969).

'A Necessary Irritant'

Banham posed the interesting paradox of whether architecture in the post-war period was tending to free itself from 'the ballast of structure' or submitting to 'the goads of mechanical service'. This represents the controversial context in which Archigram was appraised – as a liberation of architecture or an abject surrender of all that made it creative and meaningful. In his conclusion to this book he made the point that services have rendered the search for appropriate form redundant. The prioritising of services was one of the starting points for the Archigram experiment. The notion of a 'clip-on' aesthetic, a term used by Banham to refer to an outboard motor and a building philosophy evolved in the Taylor Woodrow Group for building flats, was given more force by Archigram's interest in primary structures and cybernetics.

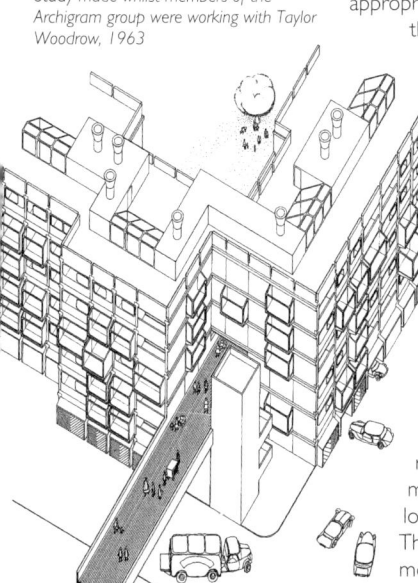

Prefabricated housing components used in a typical corner block. Part of the Fulham Study made whilst members of the Archigram group were working with Taylor Woodrow, 1963

Alison and Peter Smithson were major influences on dissident architectural students of the 1950s, particularly those they taught at the Architectural Association in London. They provided inspired teaching and combative writings whilst demonstrating how architecture could become a socially conscious post-war activity without losing a passionate commitment to modernist principles. The Smithsons defied any compromise with decorative and purely regional solutions. For the members of Archigram, they represented the point of contact with an international mainstream – evidence that British architecture was no longer provincial – 'less important than Prague or Oslo' (PC). The desire to return to the constructive optimism of early modernism is a strong theme in the work of Archigram.

Barry Curtis

THE MID 60S / ENTERING A NEW ERA

SPECIAL
Air-Cushion Vehicl

JUNE 1966 · 1s 6d

DESIGN · COMPONENTS · APPL

HOVERSHOW '66

In retrospect, it seems that the central and most hotly contested argument within architectural discourse in the 1950s was how to arrive at the best way of carrying forward modernism – whether to re-invest in vernacular, discover new analogies, follow the functional or re-interpret the founding texts.

In Architectural Design of September 1948, Siegfried Giedion expressed a fundamentalist imperative: 'The whole question can no longer be restricted to purely architectural criticism, no "new empiricism", no "cosiness" can lead us anywhere, we must go back to fundamentals.' Archigram would have been unlikely to express their views in that way; the future they were interested in was already at work in some places in the late 1950s, in engineering, utopian city planning, and in the work of like-minded architects throughout the world, but it was also to be found in the wartime projects of the 1940s (as Warren Chalk demonstrated in *Archigram* 6), and in the facts and potentialities of modern living – the Boeing 707, hovercraft, the Apollo programme and Sealab.

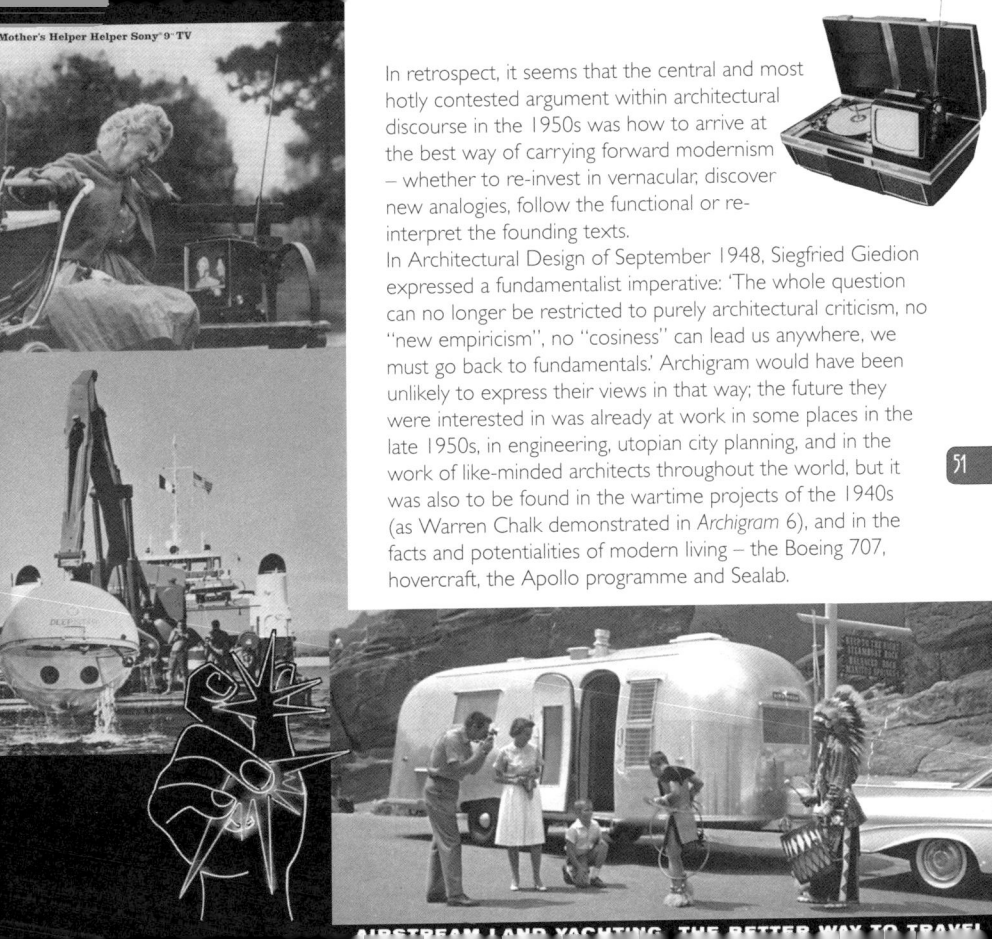

A Funny Fringe Thing: Architectural Training and Influences

Under the influence of modernism, British architectural training placed a particular significance on issues of responsibility and professionalism. Maxwell Fry – the leading member of the MARS Group, the English wing of CIAM which represented the avant-garde of modernist architecture from its foundation in 1932 – writing in 1960, but looking back to the formulations of his important book of 1944, *Fine Building*,[26] suggested that the architect, 'without adopting the distinctive role of doctor or priest, acts, or should act, in a similar capacity'. Writing as a reformed modernist in the year before the members of Archigram came together, he deplored the susceptibility of technology to military use and the forms and content of the mass media, turning away from 'the background of unorganised urban data'.[27] The writings of the first generation of modernists are full of these counsels of moderation and resistance to Americanism. In 1944, in *Architecture Arising*,[28] Howard Robertson warned against the 'intransigence, the progressive intoxication' of modernism and reminded young architects of the importance of national characteristics in building.

The formative experiences of the Archigram group were diverse but all the members shared a delight in innovation and eclecticism. To an extent membership of Archigram involved a decision not to build, to perpetuate the energies of youthful architectural-school projects and to follow the logic of constant experiment. In their various trainings they encountered some of the rigid orthodoxies of the architectural establishment and the dullness of the syllabus. Dennis Crompton felt that 'modernism had been degraded to the Georgian system and the pattern book'. Warren Chalk, as late as 1968, referred to architecture as 'a profession which is still immersed in monuments of bricks and mortar and tile hanging'.[29]

26 Maxwell Fry: *Fine Building* (Faber, London 1944).

27 Maxwell Fry: *Art in a Machine Age* (Methuen, London 1969).

28 Howard Robertson, op. cit.

29 Warren Chalk, op. cit.

'A Necessary Irritant'

Within the art school system, which was vibrant with change and open to influences from popular culture, architecture was a fringe activity. The vitality of Archigram speaks to the capacity of its members to maintain contact and exchange ideas with the artistic mainstream.

The three older members were integrated into the private and public sectors. Dennis Crompton trained at Manchester University, in a technologically based department. He then worked for Frederick Gibberd before joining the London County Council. Later, in 1964–5 whilst working for Alex Gordon and Partners he learned about prefabrication and light-weight structures from the IBIS (Industrial Building in Steel) project. Ron Herron, who trained at the Brixton School of Building and was eventually employed by the LCC, had some previous experience of working with prefabrication for the Royal Air Force. Warren Chalk was at Manchester School of Art; he met Ron Herron in 1955. In 1957, Ron Herron with Peter Nicholls, designed Starcross Secondary School for the LCC Schools Division – it was Le Corbusier influenced and used a 'movement-organising' concourse bridge which suggests some reference to the work of the Smithsons and an early indication of Archigram's interests in communication and three-dimensionality.

Model and prototype for the IBIS project. Alex Gorgon and Partners, 1964–65

Prospect (renamed Starcross) School, LCC 1955–58

For each of the members there was a similar inspirational element – access to teachers who were able to make

connections with the heroic years of modernism: for Ron Herron this role was fulfilled by Julius Poesner, contemporary of the great modernists and bibliographer of the modern movement, who taught at Brixton; for Peter Cook it was Arthur Korn, author in 1926 of *Glas im Bau und als Gebrauchsgegenstand*; and for David Greene it was Buckminster Fuller, who briefly taught at the architectural school in Nottingham. Herron testifies to 'the exhilaration of integrating knowledge by cross-referencing apparently disparate phenomena like Le Corbusier and Josephine Baker'.

Each of the Archigram group valued a shared process of autodidacticism and the frisson of crossing cultural boundaries. They explored the repressed elements of the history of the modern movement, the work of architects like Prouvé and Chareau as well as the architectures of engineering and fantasy. Peter Cook remembers an almost metaphysical yoking together of elements: 'Warren Chalk was collecting comics and I was reading 'Fruhlicht' … and at the same time we were looking at Duiker.' This enterprising and absorbing interest in the history of the modern movement and its legacy in the experimental architecture of the world, accessed through the pages of *L'Architecture d'Aujourd'hui*, was simultaneously pursued with an immersion in American popular culture. (Peter Cook remembers Ron and Warren buying Ivy League suits at Austins in Shaftesbury Avenue and looking for a while like Steve McQueen and George Raft.)

For Ron Herron there was a strong involvement in the early postwar culture of American comics and movies; he read Miller, Dos Passos and Kerouac and in most respects was more learned than the 'angry young men' of the English literary scene, with whom Archigram were occasionally compared. Los Angeles was particularly important, as was the prolific productivity of Madison

Avenue, Detroit and Hollywood, the same trinity which had been so productively explored by the Independent Group a decade previously. In this respect they were beneficiaries of what Lawrence Alloway had called 'the long front of culture',[30] freed from the critical duties of classification and discrimination into a productively catholic cross-referencing.

30 Lawrence Alloway: 'The Long Front of Culture', *Cambridge Opinion* 17, 1959.

The art school culture of the 1950s was important to the group members. Peter Cook perceived architecture as 'a funny fringe thing', but there was a network of mutual curiosity between the architectural schools. When Cook first came to the Architectural Association he was made aware of *Polygon* magazine, edited by John Outram and published at Regent Street Polytechnic, where Mike Webb was being taught at the time by James Stirling and Kenneth Frampton. *Polygon* had a more conventional appearance than *Archigram* was to have, but the spirit of its editorials indicated a similar radical project –

'Structural invention equals great architecture. STRUCTURAL WIRE WALKING EQUALS SUPER ARCHITECTURE'

– and a similar rejection of the declining modernism evident in British architecture: 'the trend is to functional tradition; bollards and granite setts, black and white paint. The Sheerness dockyard and the English vernacular are rammed down our throats while the

Perusing the plans and sections on the pages that follow, discerning architects will discover evidence of James Stirling's continuing research into the celebrated occasions of our time

Alvin Boyarsky's witty graphical comment when reviewing Stirling's Cambridge History Faculty, Architectural Design, *October 1968*

Barry Curtis

contemporary fringe play with their wavy canopies and funny roofs.'[31]

Warren Chalk's brother was a painter at the Royal College of Art and edited an issue of *Ark* magazine; through him there was close contact with artists and designers. *Ark* was highly innovative, and by the mid 1950s had already achieved the look which became familiar as a new typography and layout for the popular press in the early 1960s. The art college milieu was highly influential in the development of the characteristic graphic style of *Archigram*, and new reprographic techniques, bolder graphics and new devices like Zippertone and felt-tipped pens helped determine a style which was startlingly innovative in the realm of architectural magazines. Theo Crosby and Reyner Banham also provided contacts and opportunities to meet visitors like Yona Friedman and Richard Meier, Richard Smith and Mark Lancaster.

In general, the conventional training of the architectural schools failed to match the sense of urgency and necessity of the times, the experience of 'living in a culture that was somehow exploding' (DG). It offered versions of modernism which were still imbued with various formalisms and closely hemmed in by the realpolitik of professional practice. For young, popularly culturalised architects the syllabus seemed to be too concerned with the hardware of building and not enough with the revolutionary potentials of what Richard Neville was later to call 'playpower'[32] and what Jeff Nuttall was to describe as 'bomb culture'.[33] The architects who were to come together in editing *Archigram* shared a conviction that architecture needed to address ideas that were current at the time – new media, TV, colour magazines, the astonishingly fast developments in technology prompted by the Cold War, and the modernising of morality and sensibility which was motivated by, and enabling of a highly visible youth culture. The new technology

31 *Polygon* (Regent Street Polytechnic, 1961).

32 Richard Neville: *Playpower* (Jonathan Cape, London 1970).
33 Jeff Nuttall: *Bomb Culture* (MacGibbon & Kee, London 1968).

'A Necessary Irritant'

challenged architecture because it promised constant change, new experiences and a high degree of self-sufficiency and independence for the intelligent consumer.

Archigram combined the impulse to integrate architecture with the everyday world of packaging and electronics in a 'post-scarcity culture', whilst at the same time drawing on the most advanced technology of the space race to prepare their clients for the same kind of autonomy on earth that spacemen might enjoy on other planets. John Berger's phrase 'vertical invaders', coined to describe the newly intrusive, classless medianiks of the 1960s, takes on a new significance in the work of Archigram – the new culture of communicatory fun, education and leisure was to be transmitted from above. The nomads of the future would roam the earth with the same lack of commitment to possession and place as an interplanetary traveller. Like the Italian futurists, whose work they reprised for a 'second machine age', they presented themselves as 'primitives of a new sensibility'. Although Archigram learned from brutalism and the international impulse towards 'megastructural' architecture, they also betrayed a lighter, ironic interest in the limits of architectural discourse which was very much of the time. Their considerable learning and sophisticated awareness of the history of architecture and the state of technology were worn lightly in the highly visible realm of magazines, articles and exhibitions.

The Brain. A functioning model of sensory mechanisms, developed by The Upjohn Company, 1961.

Barry Curtis

Anything is Probable – Archigram in the 1960s

Archigram – the publication – spanned the 1960s. Although the group and the individual work of its members have had a persistent influence on the work of architects since, Archigram as a compound œuvre/image/idea has come to be closely associated with that decade. Using cheap offset litho and xerography, and screen printed with five-colour covers, *Archigram* was selling 1,000+ copies by issue 9. Indebted to popular graphics and to the contemporary pop avant-garde, it was distributed through a network of contacts at art and architectural schools and sustained by a dialogue between architects from many countries. The journal itself and its editors were transported by the timely arrival of cheap jet travel and an international network of university faculties, galleries and cultural venues. The Boeing 707 – which first flew in 1954 and which Archigram extolled as 'a flying cinema, 150 people, 600 miles per hour, 5 miles high'[34] – took them on travels and tours comparable with those of contemporary pop groups. In 1963 it carried Reyner Banham to the USA with six copies of 'Zoom', *Archigram* 4, for general distribution.

Front cover and centre 'pop-up' spread of Archigram 4, 1963

34 Soundtrack of Archigram television programme, 1966.

The 1960s were, in the words of Ron Herron, 'closer to the future', a decade 'seriously dedicated to change'. Archigram were brought

'A Necessary Irritant'

35 Christopher Booker: *The Neophiliacs* (Collins, London 1969).

Front cover of Archigram 9, 1970. This issue included a packet of seeds

Barry Curtis

together as an identifiable group in 1963, two years after Peter Cook published *Archigram* 1.

1963 was an extraordinary year in which, according to Christopher Booker, 'the image of authority was collapsing on all sides'.[35] It was the year of the Profumo sex and spies scandal, the Kennedy assassination, the Great Train Robbery, the Beatles, and Harold Wilson's speech at Scarborough on the 'white heat of technology'.

Dennis Crompton remembers the exciting realisation that it was possible then to become 'a visual intellectual', and recalls the impact of Telstar, the satellite which made world television possible and brought about the passing of the stylised and dated Pathé News. Members of the group recall the sudden exciting juxtapositions, the sense of being plunged into 'a laboratory of ideas'(DC). For the 'funny fringe activity' (PC) of architecture there were new possibilities. Mike Webb refers to 'the dressing up of ideas that were current at the time', the potential of new media, notably television and colour supplements, for both of which Archigram were to construct scenarios of the future. The group were aware too of being a channel for the dissemination of rarefied and specialized architectural ideas. Their situation was described by Mike Webb as 'being part of society, but with antennae'.

The 1960s were particularly exciting for cultural producers because, for the first time, the cultural superstructure seemed to offer explanations and understandings of the whole. Archigram offered architecture-as-politics, rather than architecture in response to politics. In the words of Frederic Jameson, writing in an attempt to periodise the 1960s, 'Culture itself falls into the world, and the result is not its disappearance but its prodigious expansion to the point where culture becomes coterminous with social life in general.'[36] Cultural theory replaced the relatively discrete and refined discourse of philosophy and Archigram's manifestoes provide startling evidence of the energy and excitement generated by the wealth of intertextual reference and analogy that became possible.

The Independent Group began to describe and urge this shift from traditional humanist values at the beginning of the decade, and recognised the emergence of what Alloway described as 'the long front of culture' – a continuum within which the new generation of autodidacts could resolve the relationship between cultural interests and the pleasures of everyday life. This new, relaxed and permissive sense of an egalitarian culture provided a space where issues of value could be decided on a pragmatic and provisional basis. Science fiction provided a realm of speculation regarding new technologies, an imaginary realm within which ideas could be circulated and tested. In *Archigram* 4 (1964), sci fi was recommended to architects: '... only those imbued with respect and enthusiasm for today's wish dreams can adequately interpret them into built environments'. Archigram projects were rarely dystopian; only 'Walking Cities' suggests that some form of *tabula rasa* might be necessary for the ultimate triumph of technological rationalism. The social programme of Archigram assumed that the logic of technology would overwhelm loyalties to nation, family, heritage and the economics of ownership. It shared with most science fiction of its time the assumption that technology was the prime facilitator of social progress.

The 'future' of Archigram was, in essence, a familiar one for many scientists, social commentators, writers and 'futurologists' of the time. Reyner Banham referred to the Buchanan Report on 'Traffic in Towns' in 1963 as a 'standard urban future'. The radically different

36 Fredric Jameson: 'Periodising the 60's', in Sohnya Sayres, Anders Stephanson, Stanley Aronowitz, Fredric Jameson (eds): *The 60's Without Apology* (University of Minnesota Press, Minneapolis 1984).

Video graphic experiments by Michael Webb

37 Timothy Leary, quoted in Colin Greenland: *The Entropy Exhibition* (Routledge & Kegan Paul, London 1983).
38 Leslie Fiedler, quoted in Greenland, op. cit.
39 L Bagrit: *The Age of Automation* (Penguin, Harmondsworth 1964).

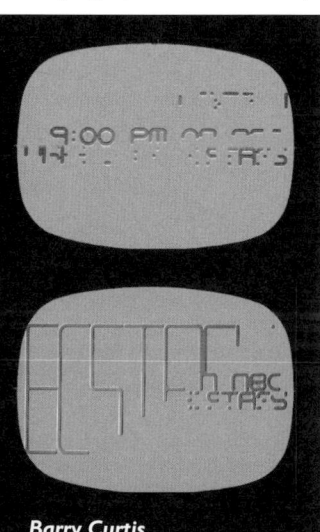

Barry Curtis

futures that were being proposed by the mid 1960s were predicated on changes which were deemed to have already happened. Timothy Leary commented that 'Human beings born after 1943 belong to a different species from their progenitors. Three new energies, exactly symmetrical and complementary – atomics, electronics and psychedelics – have produced an evolutionary mutation.'[37] Leslie Fiedler, addressing a conference on 'The Idea of the Future' in 1965, announced: 'The post-human future is here.'[38] Archigram's radical alternative futures were addressed to users who were thought to be decisively separated from the past. Bagrit, in the Reith Lectures of 1964, predicted: 'we could be moving into a golden age for most human beings'[39] and claimed that in twenty-five years the concept of charity would be obsolete as automation would support non-productive populations. Influential radical thinkers like Marcuse welcomed the benefits of complete alienation from labour which would follow the total automation of work.

The politics of Archigram resemble the politics of the counter culture, unaligned with traditional parties, libertarian, informed by considerations of ecology and selective technology. In the intensely politicised architectural contexts the group visited during their travels in the late 1960s, they were attacked by left and right. In many respects, their anarchistic individualism conforms to the neo-liberal ethos of late capitalism. The futures of Archigram imply a 'rolling back of the State', although there was evidently intended to be some untheorised mechanism of support and welfare to supply a 'standard of living package'. The society of 'control and choice' implies a politics of aggregated consumer decisions and an internalised law of reasonable co-operation.

Reyner Banham approvingly described Archigram as: 'short on

theory, long on joy'.[40] In some respects, their interest in an architecture of pleasure conformed to the quest in British post-war architecture for a populist antidote to the high seriousness of modernism, a quest which was assiduously undertaken by the organisers of the Festival of Britain in 1951. A more functional justification was the fact that vernacular precursors of mobile, prefabricated and transient structures had often been contrived for entertainment purposes. Dennis Crompton and Peter Cook had both grown up by the seaside and enjoyed the multifunctionalism and generous adaptability of resort architecture. There is a close resemblance between Archigram's conception of the continuity of amusement, learning and urban vitality, and the vision of Chtcheglov's 1953 manifesto: 'We know that the more a place is set apart for free play, the more it influences people's behaviour ... our first experimental city would largely live off tolerated and controlled tourism. Future avant-garde activities and productions would naturally tend to gravitate there. In a few years it would become the intellectual capital of the world and would be universally recognised as such.'[41]

Members of the Independent Group had been interested in Huizinga's *Homo Ludens*, published in English in the late 1940s. Huizinga testified to the emotional importance and cognitive centrality of play. Play entered into the counter culture in other ways, through absurd drama and the revitalising of Dada and surrealism, as a result of the impact of Zen thought and the political project of the Situationists. The onslaught on seriousness was compounded with a widespread rejection of the values of Protestantism and the work ethic, both of which were regarded as aspects of the superseded economy of industrial culture. Cedric Price, whose 'Fun Palace' project seems to have introduced the

40 Reyner Banham: introductory essay in Peter Cook (ed.): *Archigram* (Studio Vista, London 1972).

41 Ivan Chtcheglov, op. cit.

'A Necessary Irritant'

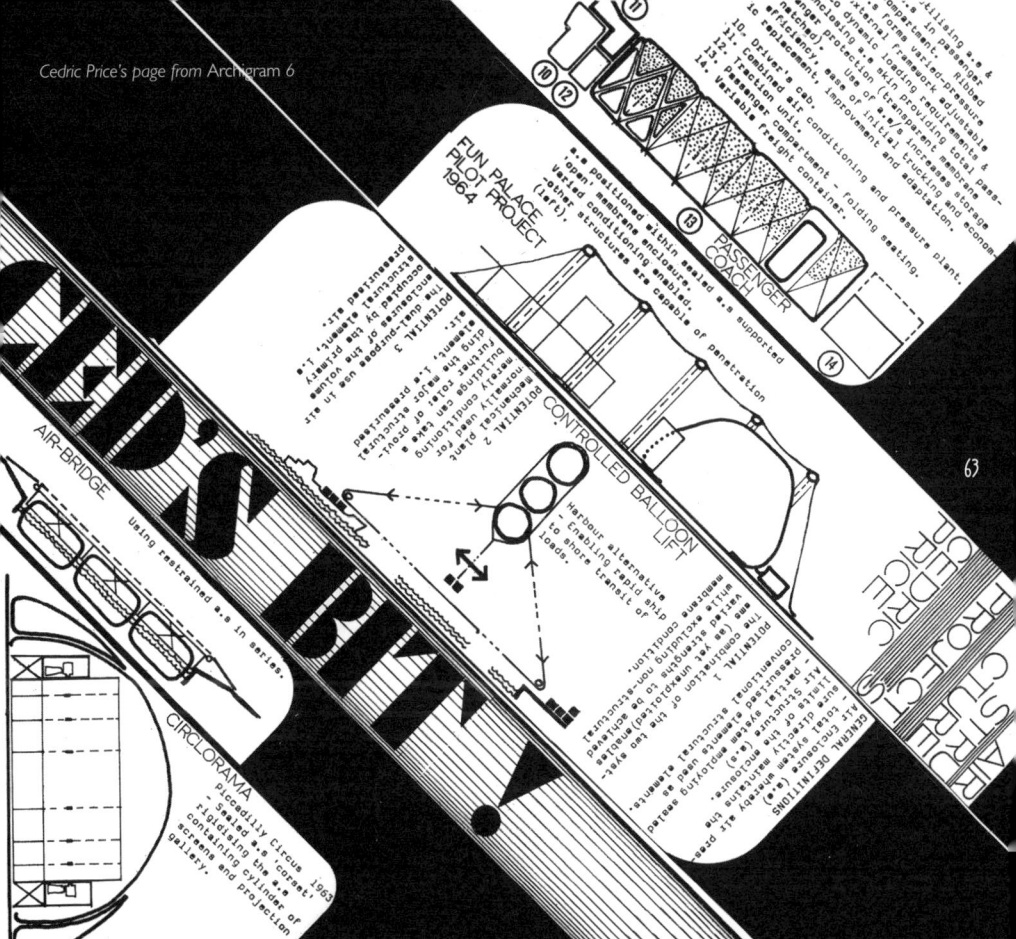

Cedric Price's page from Archigram 6

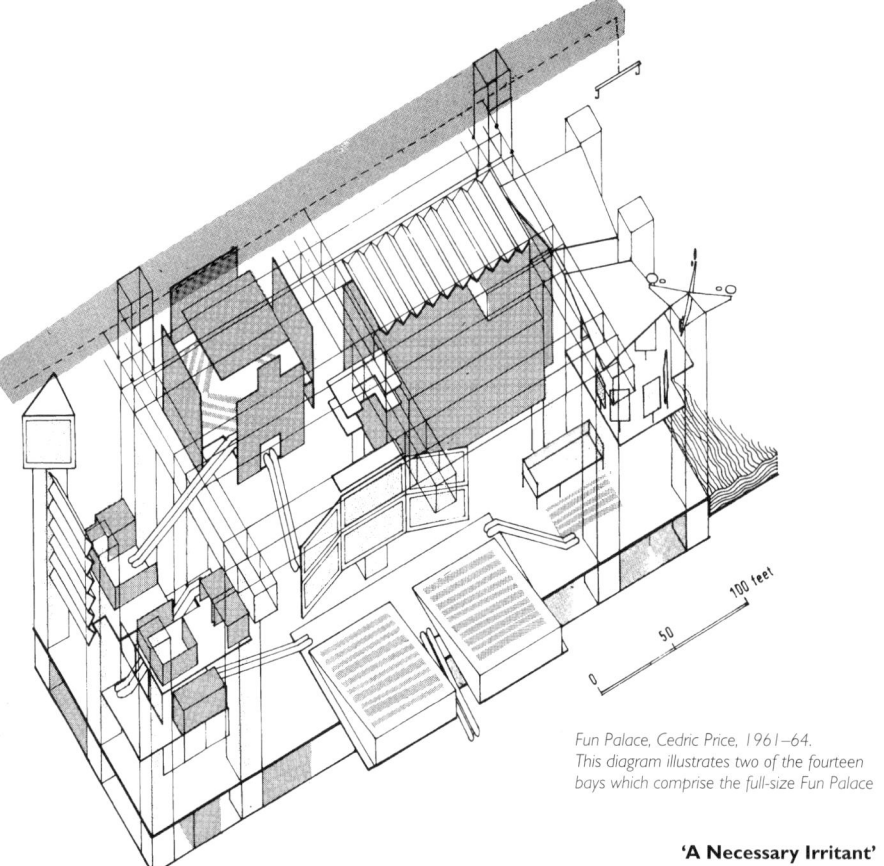

Fun Palace, Cedric Price, 1961–64. This diagram illustrates two of the fourteen bays which comprise the full-size Fun Palace

'A Necessary Irritant'

term into the architectural vocabulary, in an interview published in *Ark* 42, 1968, spoke about the resistances to a fully achieved consumer culture: 'I blame the current intellectual redefinition of Protestant morality for guilt feelings about waste and throwing things away.' The centrality of pleasure was an important component of the revolutionary impetus of the 1960s. The Hornsey students, occupying their college in 1968, protested 'against the Protestant clean, decent, self-denying, miserable glorification of work'.[42] Fun, play and pleasure were the rationale for Archigram's projects, not as recreation, the pause that refreshes, between stretches of productive labour, but as an epistemology and an end in itself.

Archigram were likened by the media to the Angry Young Men and to the Beatles. Kenneth Allsopp, the critic, identified a strategy in the work of the literary avant-garde of the 1950s of 'de-linking',[43] a persistent dismantling and re-ordering of normative social and moral values. Berenice Martin, a sociologist active in disparaging the 1960s' avant-garde, describes a comprehensive attack on what she calls 'The Kingdom of Terminus',[44] the complex system of taboos and hierarchies of 'respectable' culture – a subliminal stretching and violation of boundaries. Both perceived the disruptive interventions in spatial and structural terms.

Archigram's work was rarely angry; instead it was playfully disrespectful of existing unities. The analogies with pop are more pertinent, suggesting a revolutionary cultural strategy of inclusivity and eclecticism, a refusal to accept the sedimented logic and propriety of tradition. Archigram's rejection of architecture as a static, concrete, rule-bound activity was part of a more extensive revolt against exclusivities and aesthetic purisms. The categories established by the influential critic Clement Greenberg came under

42 Students and staff of Hornsey College of Art: *The Hornsey Affair* (Penguin, Harmondsworth 1969).

43 Kenneth Allsopp: *The Angry Decade* (Peter Owen, London 1958).

44 Berenice Martin: *A Sociology of Contemporary Cultural Change* (Basil Blackwell, Oxford 1981).

Barry Curtis

similar attack and the criteria of humanism were challenged by refusals of 'aesthetic distance', of the value of durability, or depth of meaning. Archigram were part of a wider pop exploration of the banal, commercial and camp. In other fields of cultural criticism and production there were similar formulations. In 1962, the young critics of *Movie* magazine's first issue proceeded along the same lines, setting out alternative genealogies and hierarchies by insisting on the primacy of 'style as meaning'.

The trajectory of Archigram in the 1960s followed closely that of the visual arts in a general shift of mood from the technophilia of the early years of the decade to the psychedelia of the later. It shared with pop art similar experiments with consumer culture, its objects and modes of address. After the mid 1960s there was a developing tendency towards what Lucy Lippard has characterised as 'dematerialisation'.[45] Like other artists and designers, Archigram explored minimal and conceptual ideas, the use of 'poor' materials, a concern for the landscape, primary structures and 'soft' and experiential ways of working. Although the Archigram œuvre is too complex and contradictory to reduce to a single narrative, there is a distinct move from architecture as physically massive and integrative to a scenario in which structure gives way to transportable tools, environment and states of mind.

Archigram combined a pop sensibility with an adherence to the principles of modernism's early years. Their apparently irresponsible refusal of 'architecture' incorporated a learned and conscious carrying forward of the lost modernist project of 'technological transfer'. Le Corbusier's work, which had been interpreted to endorse the formalist modern architecture of post-war Britain, could be read differently, as a visionary project which stressed building as productive rather than simply the object of production:

45 Lucy Lippard: *Six Years – The Dematerialisation of the Object* (Studio Vista, London 1973).

Living Pod, David Greene 1976

46 Le Corbusier: *Towards a New Architecture* (Architectural Press, London 1946); first published 1927.

'a house will no longer be this solidly built thing which sets out to defy time and decay ... it will become a tool as the motor car is becoming a tool.'[46] Following Banham, Archigram carefully guarded against mere aesthetic functionalism and abandoned the purist preoccupation with mechanical evolution for a model of permanent revolution. Far from conceiving the possibility of perfection in the design process, they rejected coherence and form for loose and contingent aggregation.

Cultural theory at the time, under the influence of structuralism and the New Left, was beginning to question the more mechanistic notions of determination and the hitherto inflexible relationships between base and superstructure. The structural anthropology of Lévi-Strauss and the linguistics of Saussure replaced linear narratives with the concept of the 'paradigm' and an interest in the synchronic. Notions of 'hegemony', 'articulation', 'overdetermination' and 'relative autonomy' suggest a conceptual need for both greater complexity and a more rigorous analytic technique. Structuralism indicated the possibility of a universal methodology and was capable of being transformed into an active ideology of the personal, political and historical.

L.A.W.U.N. Project No 1, David Greene 1969

In some respects, Archigram, who identified themselves as non-politically aligned, shared in the general ideology of political radicalism. They evidenced in their work a rejection of conventional authority, choosing to work as a group, occasionally working on parts of each other's projects and each representing the whole. There is an element too in their work of a Maoist shift from the political to the personal and, ironically, in the midst of their pragmatic affiliation with consumer culture and perpetual obsolescence, a radical minimising of possessions. Their preoccupation with mobility and ubiquity was often expressed in the terminologies and

Barry Curtis

ethos of 'foco' strategy and the imagery of the urban guerrilla.

The emerging counter culture, in many respects synonymous with a self-consciously post-war generation, was acutely aware of the need for alternatives to counter the rigid hierarchies of power and value which were identified in Britain with 'the Establishment'. The metaphor of 'connecting' is present within the traditional culture as a way of fitting components into an accommodating but essentially stable pantheon of value. For Archigram and the generational and cultural revolution which they came to represent, the metaphor of connection was potentially electrifying. It incorporated the sense of tapping into a new global culture, persuasively described as a 'village' by Marshall McLuhan.[47] It implied a contingent and temporary relationship, a 'plugging in' for as long as it took to transfer the charge. And it implied the sheer pleasure and productivity of the intertext, of the dissemination and miscegenation of ideas and services.

The ideology and terminology of Archigram is very much of its time. Stuart Hall, in an essay on hippies written in 1968,[48] pointed out that the new vocabulary of the emerging counter culture was prepositional, existential and emphasised the continuous present. Archigram's 'tune up, clip on, plug in' shares all of those characteristics and expresses the urgency of their need to adapt architecture to the imperatives of new cultural perceptions. In particular they sought to reduce the delays between architectural conception, building and use – a speeding up of the process out of respect for the urgency of innovative technology and in recognition of the desire for a sense of symbiotic unity.

47 Marshall McLuhan and Quentin Fiore: *War and Peace in the Global Village* (Bantam Books, New York 1968).
48 Stuart Hall: 'The Hippies: An American Moment' in Julian Nagel (ed.): *Student Power* (Merlin Press, London 1969).

'A Necessary Irritant'

QTFS – Hedgerow Village, Peter Cook 1971

49 Jim Burns: *Arthropods: New Design Futures* (Academy Books, London 1972).

50 Robert Venturi et al., op. cit.

51 Peter Cook: 'Hedgerow Village' in Peter Cook (ed.): *Archigram* (Studio Vista, London 1972).

Barry Curtis

Closer to the Future: In Conclusion

The counter culture generated ideas which were threatening to established notions of the realm and scope of architecture. The association of buildings with permanence and the centrality of tradition were fundamentally destabilised. Archigram were fascinated by 'the idea of something being there for a short time and then gone' (RH), and cited the Woodstock festival where half a million people were intensely present for two or three days. Members of the group contributed to the technology of pop concerts by pioneering work undertaken at the Light/Sound Workshop at Hornsey College of Art and to subsequent performances by the Pink Floyd. Ron Herron, inspired by such events, experimented with light shows and inflatables at UCLA. In the words of Jim Burns, in the introduction to *Arthropods*, the project was 'to find a hardware that would do the work of software'.[49]

Archigram shared too in the current dialectic of change and acceptance, finding a middle ground between the planning orthodoxies of conservation and redevelopment. Their adaptive 'tuning' prefigures the 'Main Street is nearly right' dictum of Robert Venturi and Denise Scott Brown,[50] except that in the later 1960s Archigram complemented the commercially hyperactive projects with pastoral and nomadic utopias producing a dialectic double taxonomy of urban picturesque and electrified rurality: 'no dividing line between home in a paper sleeping bag and the sophistication of the Farnsworth House'.[51]

In architectural terms there were to be serious formal consequences of this productive fragmentation. The proprieties of unity and scale were rejected. Neither the streamlined containers of heroic modernism, nor the picturesque articulations of post-war empiricism were adequate to the new interpretation of the needs of technology. For Archigram, entropy needed to be seen as part of the system and the effects of perpetual consumption and change needed to be formally recognised. The megastructural work of the early years combines a highly organised, but relatively invariant infrastructure with a constantly changing superstructure, which it only determines in the last instance. The role of the architect shifted from that of 'formgiver' to that of mechanic, ever ready to 'tune' and 'tweak' the living unit, the suburb or the whole metropolis. The telephone and the crane became the essential tools of planning. The great conceptual enablers of the megastructure were the architecture of wartime and the space race. Post-Sputnik space travel and the imaginative literature which had preceded it metaphorically freed the gravity-bound situation of architecture on earth and provided visual metaphors – satellites, probes, non-terrestrial landing and roving vehicles – which sanctioned new, ragged, unfinished and purposeful appearances.

Archigram combined a pop sensibility with a new kind of social utopianism. They reinstated components of the founding dream of modernism, insisting on the primacy of change and the possibility of living at the margins of progressive technology. They were widely anthologised as examples of the most extreme and fantastic technological futurism, but at the heart of the work is a concern for everyday life and experience, a project for bringing the pleasures and services enjoyed in some contexts into all situations and a recognition of the architect's responsibility for the whole environment: 'When it's raining in Oxford Street, the architecture is no more important than the rain, in fact the weather has more to do with the pulsation of the Living City.'[52] Archigram's interest in the basic elements of urban experience brought about a characteristic synthesis of the 'primitive' and the technologically sophisticated – a

Living City, 1963

52 Peter Cook: Introduction to the 'Living City' section of Living Arts 2, pp.68–71 (ICA +Tillotsons, London 1963).

'A Necessary Irritant'

53 Wolf Vostell and Dick Higgins: *Fantastic Architecture* (Something Else Press, nd); first published as *Pop Architektur*, Droste Verlag, Dusseldorf 1969.

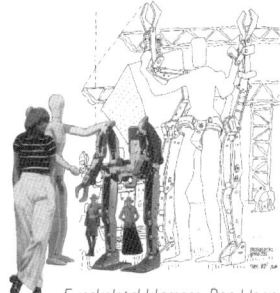

Exoskeletal Harness, Ron Herron

54 'Archigram Competition – Monte Carlo': *Architectural Design*, September 1970.

55 'Enviropill': Ron Herron, Los Angeles, April/May 1969, discussed in a lecture at Central/ St Martins, London Institute, May 1991.

'both ends against the middle' situation that is typical of 1960s' revolt. Wolf Vostell, in his book *Fantastic Architecture*,[53] called it 'a new beginning with utterly primitive artisanship and non-architecture'. The dialectic between the empirical and the transcendent leaves the question open, regarding the achievement of Archigram – whether their work is evidence of the overwhelming of architecture by technology and consumer culture, or an exemplary attempt at integrating culture, nature and science.

Archigram in general, and Ron Herron in particular, were interested in movement. They followed the logic of a particularly British futurism which suggested that the machine could constitute a paradigm, but not one that should dictate human characteristics. Herron proposed 'an architecture that twitched … was responsive to people', citing Mike Webb's 'Rent A Wall' as exemplary. The static, unresponsive nature of architecture was regarded as a skin that needed to be shed. Archigram's projects suggest the necessity of deconstruction, simulation or symbiosis: 'You can be and do anything anywhere, why shouldn't a school be a beach.'[54] Year by year through the 1960s they pursued the logic of their assault on architectural atavism, suggesting the possibilities of wearing, carrying or becoming architecture. Psychedelics indicated a possibility of the ultimate reconstruction: 'Enviropill – sit and dream it all.'[55] With projects like 'Computer City' and 'Monaco', they installed culture as a service which could be accessed or quit by the use of terminals or meters.

Archigram shared in the technological optimism of a buoyant economy which could not foresee economic entropy, mass unemployment and ecological disaster. Although their well-informed perspective on the future enabled them to predict a decline in work, the optimistic mood of the time constituted this as a 'leisure

Barry Curtis

problem'. The apparent logic of growth and technological enabled them to establish a rapport with the energies of the early twentieth century. However, they registered a distance from modernism, rejecting its aesthetics of functionalism and the purist preoccupation with mechanical evolution and object types: 'We have chosen to bypass the decaying Bauhaus image which is an insult to functionalism. The demand for functionalism is, of course, not new but one has to face that demand again and again and prevent that functionalism becoming a style.'[56]

56 Archigram 1, 1960, quoted in Peter Cook (ed.): *Archigram*, op. cit.

Archigram were engaged on two fronts in an attack on the machine aesthetic and the historicisms which they, however playfully, embedded in some of their re-tuned cityscapes. They placed little value on coherence or materials – there is no closure, components are replaceable and the 'building' is in the mind and under the control of its user. Warren Chalk looked forward to 'a much more permissive situation where people will just assemble the bits and pieces that they collect together themselves'. Peter Cook predicted a future where 'Our rooms expand infinitely. Our walls dissolve into impermeable mists or into the imagery of stories and fables and dreams. Our floors dissolve into original works of art or into hybrid combinations of furniture, road-vehicle, garden enclosure, rock, in other words even these homely things can themselves be catalysts for a very relaxed architecture.'[57]

57 Peter Cook on Archigram in 'New Theory' section of Theo Crosby: *How to Play the Environment Game* (Penguin/Arts Council, Harmondsworth 1973).

There is much in Archigram which carries forward concerns of the social architecture of the 1940s and the enhanced and totalising role of the architect/planner of that time. The heroic scope of the Archigram projects seems to be indebted to the conceptual world of total reconstruction and new beginnings. In some respects they look further back to the engineering traditions of American industrial design as it was manifested at the World Fairs of the

1930s and in the projects of the visionary urbanists of the 1920s. Archigram started the 1960s as full and inventive participants in an international exploration of the potential of megastructures. Reyner Banham surveyed the collective project and accorded them a central role: 'Having produced one of those masterly images which immortalise a moment [Plug-in City], typify their age, and so on, they spent the rest of the decade doing something else, heading in a different direction from that taken by the very movement to which that master image was most meaningful.'[58] The central paradox of Archigram's work was present in the megastructural project – an authoritarian framework which was highly permissive in terms of use. Mike Webb's earlier 'Sin Centre', intended for the site of the Empire Theatre in Leicester Square demonstrated something of the same order – a carefully constructed sub-structure supporting a visually chaotic superstructure. The 'Plug-in University' project of 1965 was conceived at a time of rapid growth in higher education but provided the potential for deconstruction when the anticipated effects of new communications technologies would make it possible for education to be broad- or narrow-cast (a persistent fantasy in the higher education of the 1990s).

58 Reyner Banham: Megastructure: Urban Futures of the Recent Past (Thames & Hudson, London 1976).

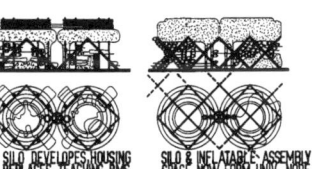

In 1966 the logic of demountability was pursued in David Greene's 'Living Pod' as a microcosmic exploration of personal space. The move towards the interchangeable capsule, pioneered by Warren

Barry Curtis

Chalk in 1964, was intended to 'bypass the myths of urban design' and to reject the notion of 'housing as a folk art'.[59] David Greene predicted: 'It is likely that under the impact of the second machine age, the need for a house (in the form of a permanent static container) as part of man's psychological make up will disappear.'[60] In the following year, 'Control and Choice' carried this proposal further, seeking to emancipate the user by finding adequate 'systems, organisations and techniques'. The architects were, effectively, writing the software which would enable the program of everyday life to run with a minimum of responsibility for self-maintenance: 'If we value person above object, can we just leave the gear with which we survive to look after itself – what a great idea, an Anarchy City!'[61] 'Ideas Circus' and 'Instant City' are agit-prop architecture intended to bring a transitory experience of urban intensity to remote towns and villages, to seed them with the potential for growth.

Increasingly, the late work of Archigram develops lighter and lighter touches – 'A Quietly Technologised Folk Suburbia' combines the modernising impulse with an appreciation of something dangerously like traditional rural values. Rock bands at the same time were rediscovering the compatabilities of psychedelia and the 'Village Green Preservation Society'. Even the densely urban project of 'Tuning' London was described as 'a forestage of enactments'. Michael Cassidy, reviewing a retrospective of Archigram at the ICA in 1973, accused them of failing to take human nature into account: 'Technological futures can only be sustained if the human futures they purport to serve are themselves valid.'[62] By 1973 the conspicuous consumption of the

59 Peter Cook: 'The Capsule', in Peter Cook (ed.): Archigram, op. cit.

60 David Greene: 'Living Pod', in Peter Cook (ed.): Archigram, op. cit.

61 Archigram Group work: 'Control and Choice', housing study and exhibit at the Paris Biennale 1967; quote from 'Expendable Place Pads' drawing, made for Control magazine.

62 Michael Cassidy, review of Archigram exhibition at the ICA in Building, 224/I, January 1973.

Simultaneous Event Facility, Ron Herron 1969

'A Necessary Irritant'

THE POSSIBILITY OF CASUAL DWELLINGS

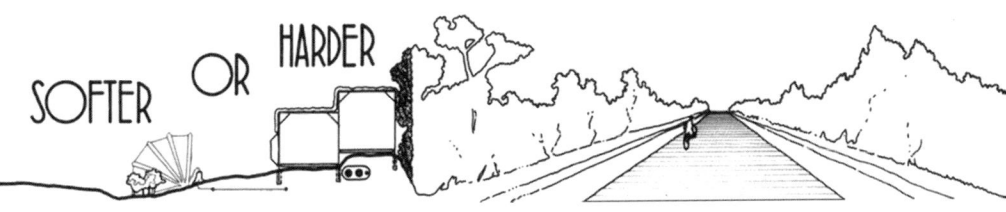

QTFS – Hedgerow Village, Peter Cook 1971

1960s was beginning to be called into question. The Apollo programme had been temporarily suspended, the oil crisis presaged the end of 'non scarcity', a conference on world ecology was planned in Stockholm, and there were early signs of a rejection of 'the future' in favour of the past. Archigram's conspicuous success at the beginning of the 1970s was marked by their setting up a permanent office and hiring staff. Although the individuals continued to develop their ideas and to practise successfully throughout that decade, they found themselves in a less sympathetic environment for collaborative visionary projects.

A number of recent architectural developments have focused new attention on Archigram. The successes of Norman Foster and Richard Rogers have established an interest in the genealogy of 'high tech' that clearly locates Archigram as a precedent. Michael Sorkin, tracing back the legacy of Richard Rogers, finds it in: 'a

Barry Curtis

Pool enclosure for Rod Stewart, Ascot, Archigram Architects 1972

branch of that history which threads its way from Paxton and Brunel, through Sopwith and Spitfire, to the Meccano-strewn nursery of the architect'.[63] Archigram have, however, tended to find structures like the Pompidou Centre, which they so clearly influenced, disappointingly static and uni-functional. Although some 'deconstructionist' architecture is visually similar to such projects as 'Plug-in City', the concern which Archigram showed for function and modularity clearly differs from the formalisms of much post-modern work.

63 Michael Sorkin: 'Richard Rogers, Lloyds and Others', in Exquisite Corpse: Writing on Buildings (Verso, London 1991).

'A Necessary Irritant'

Adventure Playground, Milton Keynes, Archigram Architects 1972

64 Nigel Coates: 'Gamma Manifesto' in 'Gamma City' issue of NATO (NATØ and Architectural Association, London 1985).

Barry Curtis

Narrative Architecture Today (NATØ) – a British avant-garde group of the 1980s – does bear some interesting relationships to Archigram, although in some ways it was very critical of the cool and objective position of pop and reluctant to identify with the discredited futurism of the 1960s: 'Customise situations with new means and new technologies, not as futurology, but as taking stock.'[64] But NATØ was at one with Archigram on the need to retain the complexity of the urban experience, and both were susceptible to the 'lure of the primitive' and the nomadic. Where they differed was in the contrasting nature of the architectural politics of the two decades. Archigram conceived themselves as a particle of the future, integrating figuratively, and sometimes literally, from above. NATØ, affiliated to the sub-cultural activities of punk, sought to infiltrate and subvert. Instead of an architecture which could act as an induction into new states of mind, NATØ aspired to an architecture which reflected the real life of the apocalyptic city: 'Architecture as experience, architecture which accepts the software of signing on and collecting cheques.'[65]

Archigram combined a number of projects for architecture and the architect. In some respects their projects are poetic enterprises, in others they are ambitious social interventions with the architect functioning as a guerrilla/engineer. Tafuri has said that one of the aims of the recent avant-garde is to validate itself through the media, and it was certainly one of Archigram's projects to inject noise into the system. From a time of recession, pessimism and entropy it is difficult not to blame Archigram for misreading the future, for being naive about capitalism's capacity to recuperate radical ideas, for neglecting the the persistence of greed and the dynamic forces consuming desire.

Like many theorists of the time, Archigram's concept of need and want was rational rather than fantastic. They projected the benefits of enjoying a symbiotic and empowering relationship with the environment to such an extent that the renunciation of fetishised objects, land and

65 Christina Norton: 'On the Boardwalk', in 'Albion – Straight from the Heart' issue of NATO (NATØ and Architecural Association, London 1983).

Transformation of a South Kensington Street Corner, Addhox, Peter Cook 1970

'A Necessary Irritant'

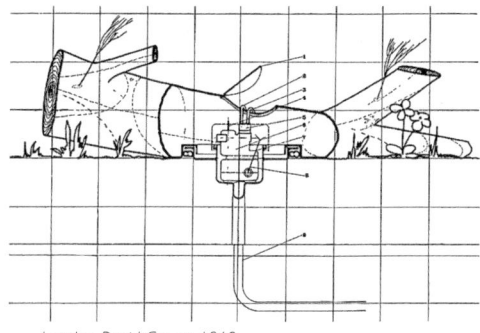

Logplug, David Greene 1969

inheritance was axiomatic. We need to accept that we are further from the future than they were. The aspect of their work which continues to have a strong appeal is its resistance to closure – its rejection of the centripetal. They were passionately concerned for growth and education, interested in providing the tools and 'kits of parts' which would enable their clients to become their own self-realising architects.

In his essay on Richard Rogers, in which he makes claims for the values of his work as a synthesis of technology and form, Michael Sorkin sums up the history of Archigram in three sentences – two admiring and one cautionary – suggesting as he does, the penalty of marginalisation that has to be paid for transgressing too fundamentally the conventions of architecture: 'In Archigram's trajectory ... the line is traced from gigantism and statical heroics to invisibility, to the telephone jack in the trunk of the tree. It's a courageous argument, this lunge to invisibility; one which recognizes the real spatial consequence of networking technologies, their actual ageographia, far more succinctly than any recapitulation of high Victorian tech. But its also suicidal.'[66] Reyner Banham recognised, in 1960, the difficulty of the incredible expanding project in which Archigram were engaged. At the end of his seminal revaluation of modernism and its relation to technology he sketched the challenge which was taken up by Archigram at the beginning of that optimistic decade: 'The architect who proposes to run with technology knows that he will be in fast company, and that, in order to keep up, he may have to emulate the futurists and discard his whole cultural load, including the professional garments by which he is recognised as an architect.'[67]

66 Michael Sorkin, op. cit.

67 Reyner Banham: Theory and Design in the First Machine Age (Architectural Press, London 1960).

Barry Curtis

Peter Cook's Archigram Entr'Acte – 2
Capsules, Pods and Skins

The creation of a style or a set of imitable mannerisms is one thing, but the creation of typologies is altogether more intriguing. Archigram projects have always been to do with designing things, very few have been exercises in abstract rhetoric or to do with propositions that remained as diagrams.

Ideas about cities and living in the immediate future, ideas about combining transportation and furniture, ideas about the interchangeability of parts, ideas about the metamorphosis of one object into another — all of these demanded prototypes or mutations of known typologies. The 'capsule' became a convenient term with which to discuss the perfected, industrially-designed prototype home — with the space capsules somewhere in the background, creating the necessary rhetoric but also calling to mind the concept of totally interrelated parts and appliances.

Buckminster Fuller was the godfather of the concept, the space capsule the outrider, and the capsules of Kisho Kurakawa (seen by members of Archigram in issues of Architecture d'Aujourd'hui) the

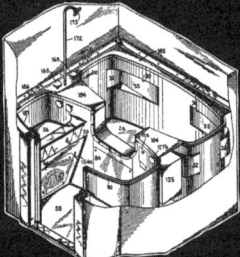
Bathroom Unit, Buckminster Fuller

Osaka Capsule, Kisho Kurakawa

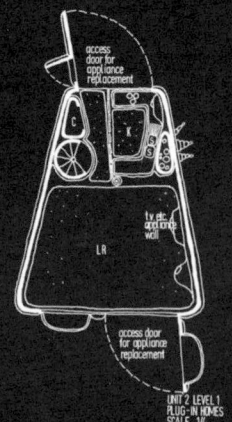
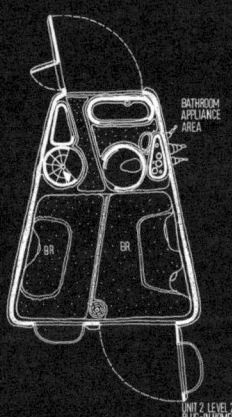

Capsules, Pods and Skins

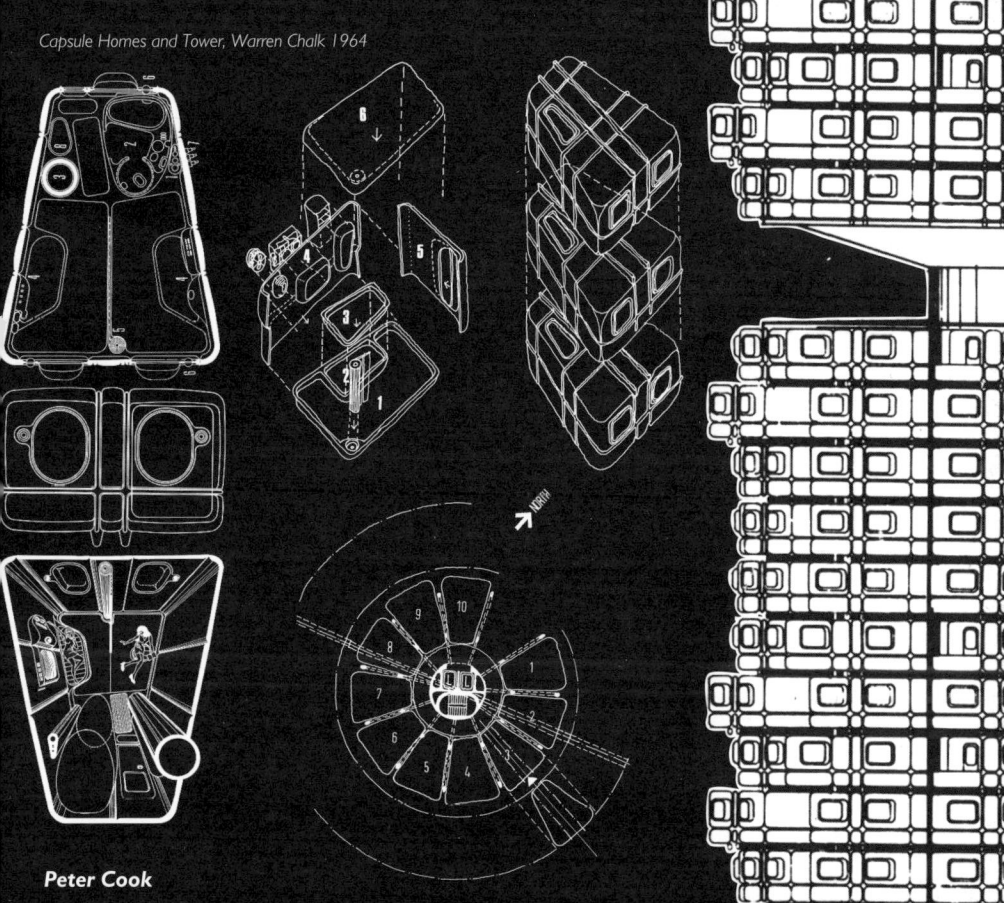

Capsule Homes and Tower, Warren Chalk 1964

Peter Cook

ones to beat! Warren Chalk developed his wedge-shaped capsules with a completely integrated set of components and, with Ron Herron, developed the idea of making the capsule out of a series of strips or 'gaskets'. The basic idea remained, but an instinct to 'flex' the system was already under way.

Mike Webb's 'home' projects were always looser – bed pods and bath pods occurred on various versions of the Auto-Environment, but so too did folding screens, openwork floor gridding, vehicles, and a general proposition of interchangeability. With Webb the implication was always that of a more ambient and more delicate rethink of the idea in its next manifestation. Thus the Auto-Environment became the Cushicle and Suitaloon and then Dreams Come True.

An underlying power of the Group was definitely the nudging effect of one member moving just that bit further than before and offering an unspoken challenge to the others in the development of an idea-run. More often than not, Webb was the most far-out (and occasionally the most obscure), but the challenge could come from just about any corner.

Webb and I were able to work at the Hornsey College of Art on the idea of the electric car as part of a future environment. More and more the notion developed that bits of the 'home' could be hybrids between building component and

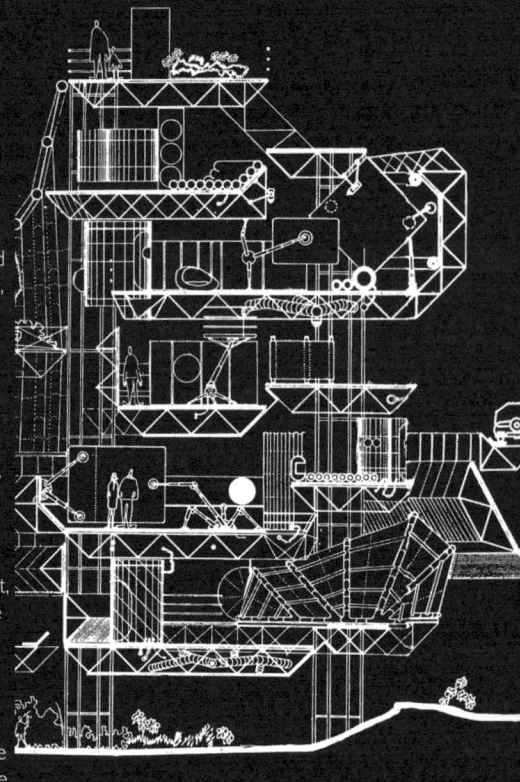

Capsules, Pods and Skins

Control and Choice Dwellings, Warren Chalk, Peter Cook, Dennis Crompton, Ron Herron, 1967

Peter Cook

furniture, between 'robot' and appliance, appliance and room, room and furniture, and round again!

The Ideas Circus and the Instant City began to melt away the 'city' – at least for a while. The relatively early Blow-up Village, and certainly the many notions of Ron Herron – Manzak, Enviro-Pill, The Electronic Tomato – as well as the larger schemes, were all probes into a disintegrative set-up less like a city with housing and more like an exploded dodgem-car pad.

The real challenge (and it was inevitable) was towards the neat idea of 'the room' – a challenge to the whole issue of 'enclosure' itself and thus a fairly fundamental dig at the whole inherited architectural portmanteau.

Auto-Environment, Michael Webb 1964–66

As early as 1961, David Greene and I were talking about 'skins' in Archigram 1, and trying to make a waywardly folded translucent skin for our version of the Lincoln Civic Centre competition. This skin had scatterings of little bubbles in it – blisters (or were they appropriated dome lights?). We had to wait some years to see glass and plastics technology that could realise such a gentle skinning.

Webb's Sin Centre had a wonderful skin that cascaded down to form a 'roof-is-wall' proposition. I am sure that the first model of the Living City structure (though more deformed) was sub-conscious homage to the Webb piece. A while later, however, these two leading devices – the capsule and the draped skin – became inevitable partners and, along with ramps, balloons, cars and robotics,

Capsules, Pods and Skins

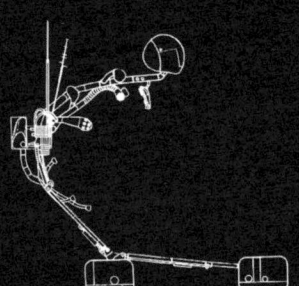 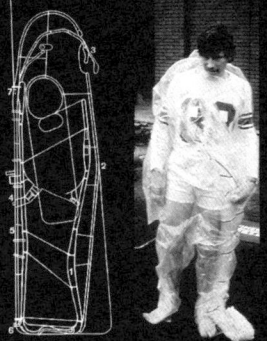 

Cushicle, Michael Webb with David Greene model, 1966

an inevitable set of props for large-scale Archigrammic coverage. The capsules defined and serviced special needs, the skins kept the weather out – and all sorts of tricks and meanderings in between were then possible. The idea of 'scatter' – heard maybe from the Smithsons or Price – was a heady possibility developed out of these few ingredients and, of course, the many hybrids that they themselves could generate.

The 'bugged' wall anticipated the advent of 'smart' glass. The robotics anticipated the increase in automation linked to electronics. The skins and folds were in anticipatory spirit with the computer-generated folds of the 1990s.

Key to the Archigram spirit, however, was a certain looseness and irritation with ossification – perhaps even a shying-away from setting series of 'rules' for the parts, a reluctance to set hierarchies or to fix sequences. The establishment of a 'kit' of robotised elements for the Monte Carlo project was essential, but the main point of them was their ability to operate in any juxtaposition. So the identification of characteristic parts should always be taken as a series of clues or steps, with the inevitable next step being just beyond – the car about to melt into a pad, the skin about to become a mere air condition (see Webb's Brünhilde's Magic Ring of Fire), the capsule about to fragment into a virtual miasma of little gizmos.

Capsules, Pods and Skins

Brünhilde's Magic Ring of Fire, Michael Webb 1968

Peter Cook

Archigram Classic
ENTERTAINMENTS CENTRE, LEICESTER SQUARE, LONDON

Michael Webb, Thesis Project : Regent Street Polytechnic. London
1959, modified, 1960, 61, etc.

This project (also known as the Sin Centre) became a *cause celebre* from several points of view: a daring concept whereby the normally separated elements of showtime audience and parked cars are brought together on the inclined plates that develop from the winding ramp system. The ductwork sprouts like magic from the cores (you can see the result of this device in the interior of of Gunther Domenig's 'Z' Bank in Vienna). The Polytechnic failed the scheme and continued to do so several times even after its prominent display at MOMA and published status as an epoch-making and original technic icon.

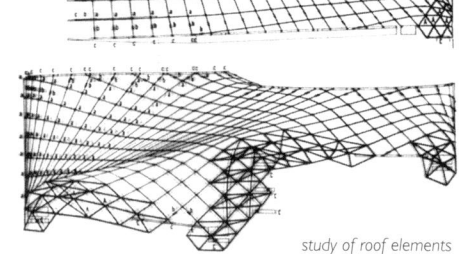

study of roof elements

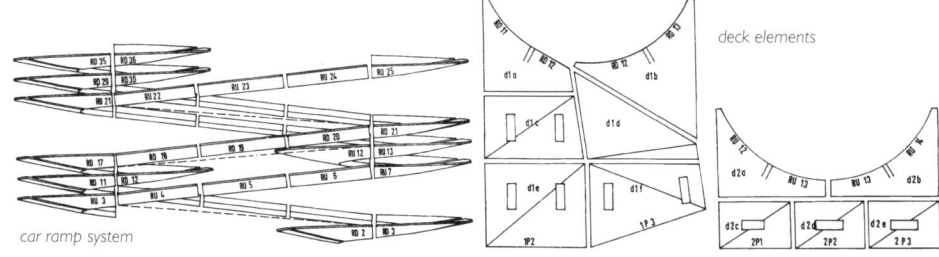

deck elements

car ramp system

Sin Centre

studies of access ramps and parking decks

linking of helical stair/ramp units

composite plan of pedestrian decks, car ramp and access system

crossover

Michael Webb

plan with Leicester Square at bottom

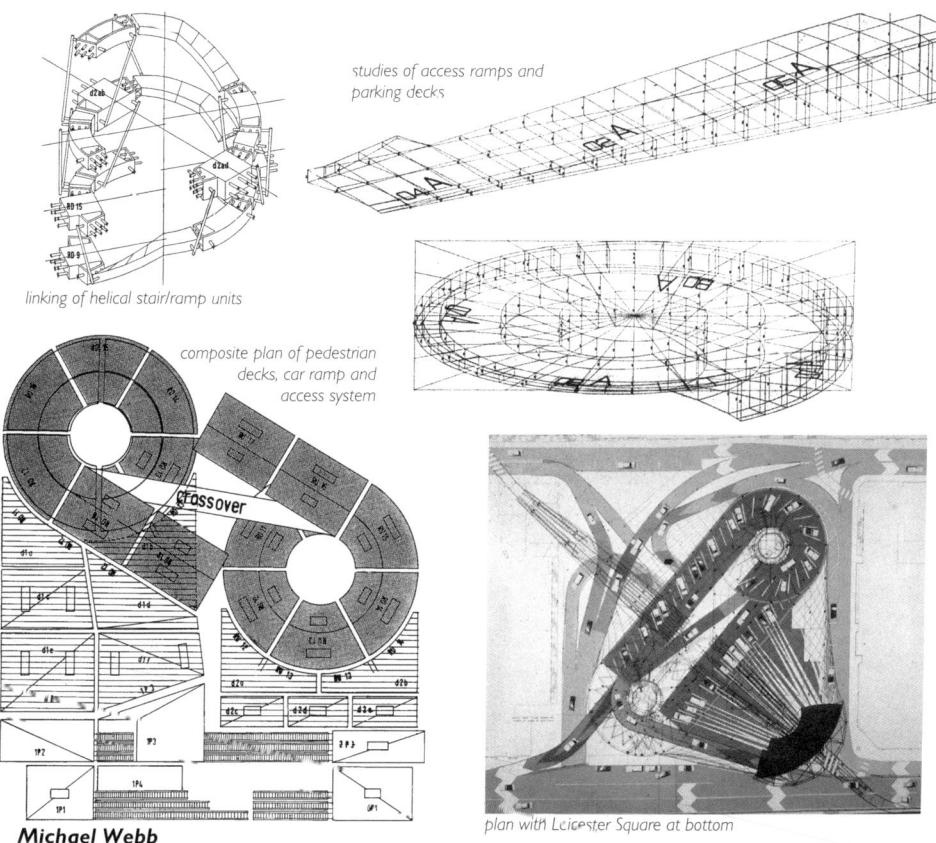

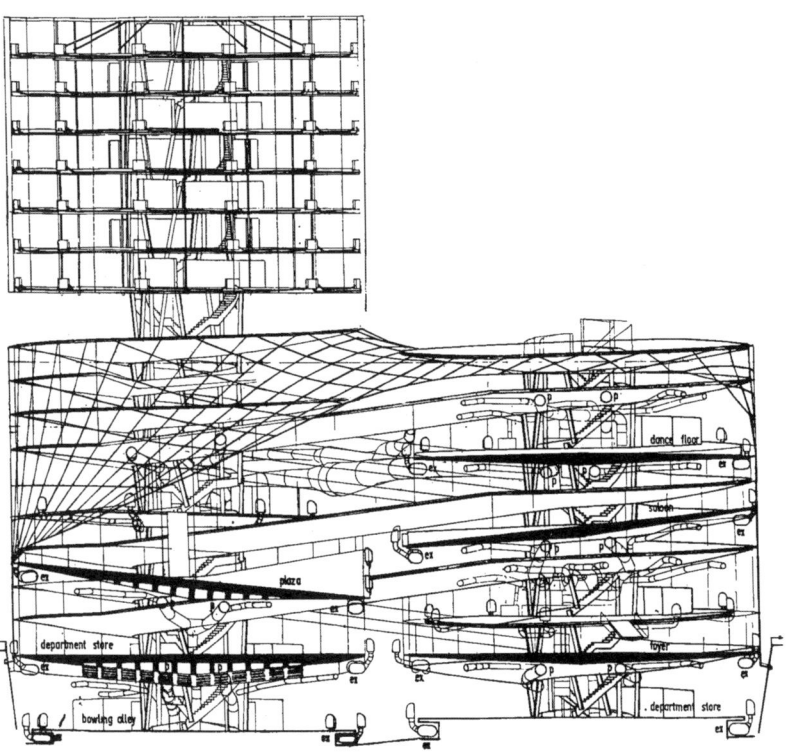

cross section

Sin Centre

diagrammatic perspective of the interior of the building with its suspended covering of plastic sheets and steel cables

Michael Webb

Archigram Classic
ENTERTAINMENTS TOWER, MONTREAL

Peter Cook (Designed for Taylor Woodrow Construction Ltd) 1963

Taylor Woodrow asked their special design group (headed by Theo Crosby and including for a time *all* members of the Archigram Group) to make an internal competition for a tower that could exploite their spun concrete television tower as the core of a feature for the upcoming Montreal World's Fair. The Cook design was chosen and developed along with the making of the model by Dennis Crompton. An observatory, restaurant and exhibition centre that could be used after the Fair were linked diagonally.

The diagonalised exhibition area was, effectively, a prototype for the 'Plug-in City'.

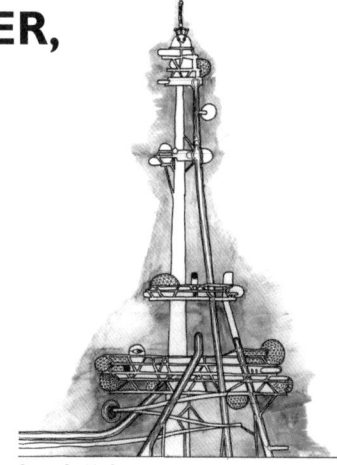

Peter Cook's first version

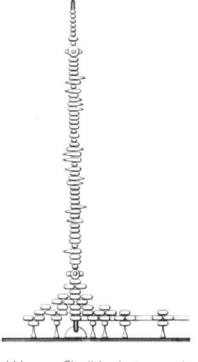

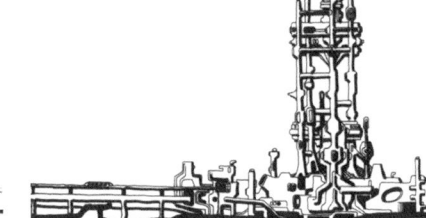

Warren Chalk's design and ... Ron Herron's

Montreal Tower

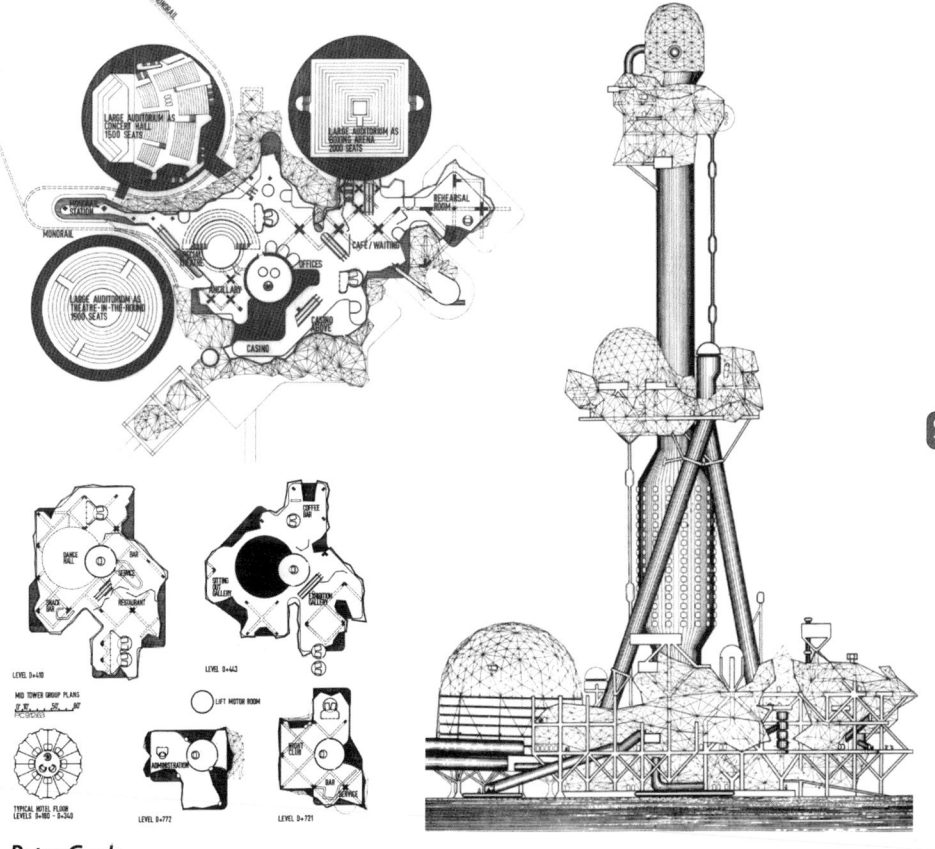

Peter Cook

Montreal Tower

How tricky to write of endless schemes both naive and new when not for Titipu: naive, as they seem now; new, meant not so much in the temporal sense of the word, but more as pertaining to a lasting condition of bizarreness and unfamiliarity. Thus can it be applied to a scheme dating from 64; unable to leave anything I've done alone......here follows some more fiddling around in an article entitled:

A Longtime Devotion to the Notion of Motion.

motion in buildings..specifically, motion involving their major tectonic components: the only parts of an ordinary building that move regularly are its windows (rotating around a vertical axis or sliding up and down).......
.... and its doors (rotating around a vertical axis........ So if these components were to be just windows and doors, then when occupied the building would be constantly on the move. It doesn't, like other buildings.. sit around doing nothing.

I might lift this paraphrase from "The Mikado" and use it instead,perhaps more appropriately, to commence another article entitled :
"Concepts of Infinity related to Perspective Projection"

The Notion of Motion

First stage: 64

Square steel floor and ceiling plates hinged together in 4 packs, still toasty from an on site manufacturing unit(!), roll along track ways in the sky, unfolding like a petal....a metal petal.

These four images form a storyboard sequence for an animation, showing the unfolding. Per spective projection is used...so as to allow sky gradation from zenith to horizon....thus establishing up-and-down. The Prince of Rays i.e. the center of vision...is perpendicular to the face of one of the floor plates, and remains so while the plate unfolds.

```
image 1:   floor plate slides along trackway.
image 2:   underneath it, looking vertically.
image 3:   upside down, looking horizontally.
image 4:   on top, looking vertically down.
```

The plan shows the plates fully deployed, as Bucky used to say. Doors and windows, hinged at both sides, some transparent, some opaque

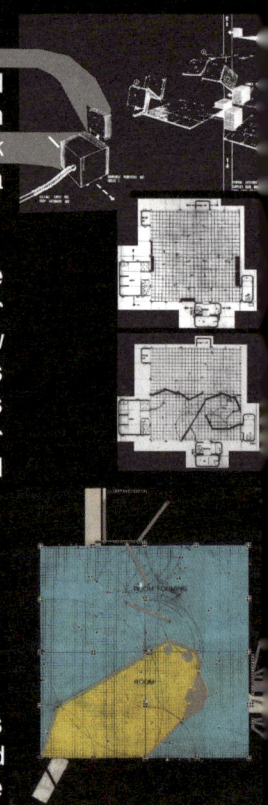

The Notion of Motion

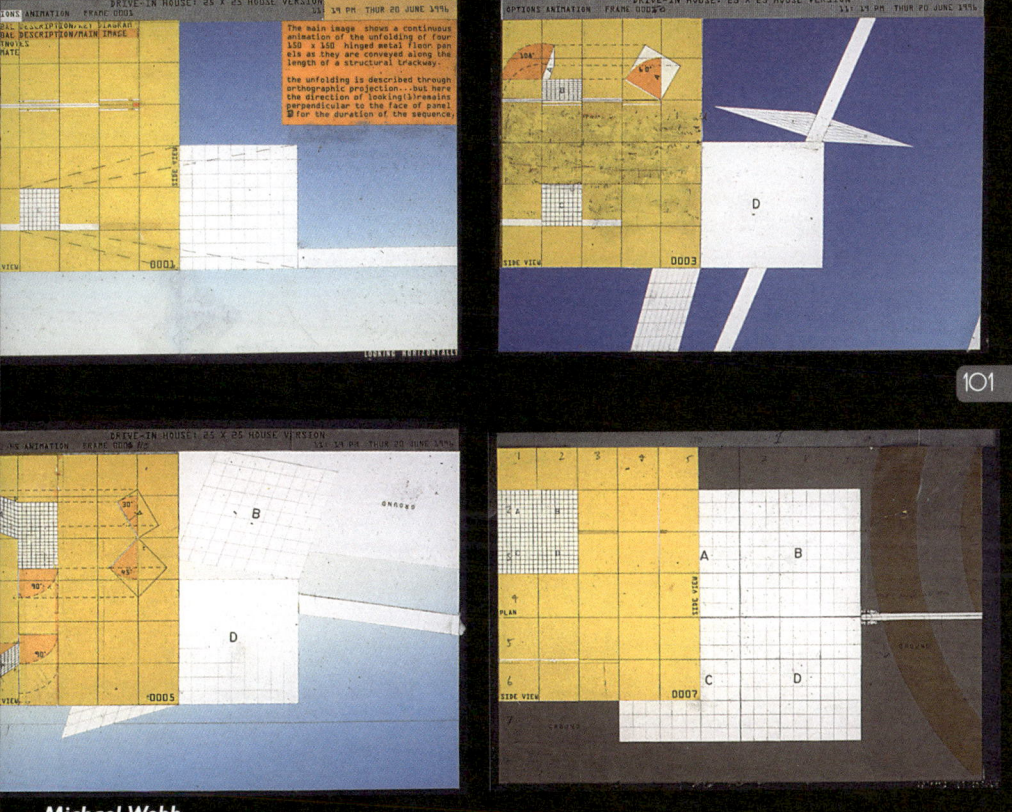

Michael Webb

some insulated, can swing around so as to de
form or form spaces.
The spaces are serviced by SSUs......sliding
bathrooms, kitchens and closets

76 version.

SSUs become miniaturised and subsumed within
opening and shutting window and door panels.
So: compose spaces according to what you fig
ure you'll want to get up to in that space.

The Rent-a-Wall drawing was done with the in
tention of suggesting how a scheme like this
could be marketed.

From 72:
"Its possible to see the interior space of a
a car as a house of reduced interior volume
to which wheels and a motive power unit have
been attached. A suit of clothes with match
ing hat could represent a further reduction
in size. In fact, in the USA, what with TV,
cigarette lighter, quadraphonic soundarround
front seats sliding up and down.. as well as

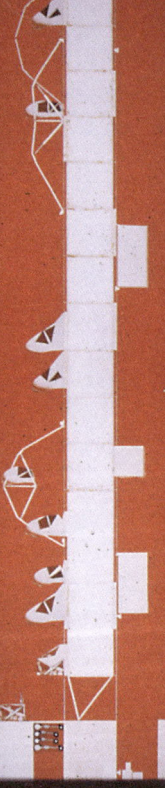

The Notion of Motion

"Today's homes are little more than a place to sleep next to one's car"
George Bernard Shaw

Already there! from "Ode to a Nightingale " by Keats suggested to me the ability of computer animation as well as poesy to transcend pesky little problems like gravity or time.

Michael Webb

forward and backward....the car is better appointed and certainly more admired than its owner's own living room....and yet out there in the 'burbs this example of vita domestica sits unused in the driveway for most of the day."

In the Sky-Rise scheme non-standard cars arrive at the base of the slab, where body and chassis separate, the chassiss to be stacked in underground storage racks, the bodies to be lifted via crane to the appropriate apartment in the sky, or, perhaps more excitingly to the inappropriate apartment.

Already there! car and apartment open up to become one! one space i.e.

On the other side of the slab room settings are constructed and hoisted up via crane to make additional space.

In the Cushicle/Suitaloon scheme the suit of clothes with matching hat is now executed in inflatable mylar, and inflates to become the

house, now of regular interior volume....the
wheels are now air cushion pads.

Suits for Dave and Pat feature a string bag
-like arrangement with orange heating coils,
drawn closed at the knee: notice the neck of
the bag in yellow. When Dave and Pat decide
to get together they touch knees and shortly
thereafter find themselves inside one rather
large suit.

In the third image Dave enters the house bit
just as he en..got together with Pat.   Dave
touches the house's inflatable knee and ....
shortly thereafter finds himself inside. His
suit is now part of the skin of the house...
along with the rest of his wardrobe: tuxedo,
leisure wear etc.

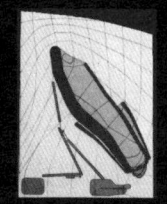

In this Cushicle drawing the points at which
the grid intersects with the lines that comp
rise the image remain stationary in relation
to that image...as the Cushicle unfolds. Did
you get that? So they become very distorted.

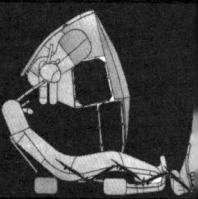

The Notion of Motion

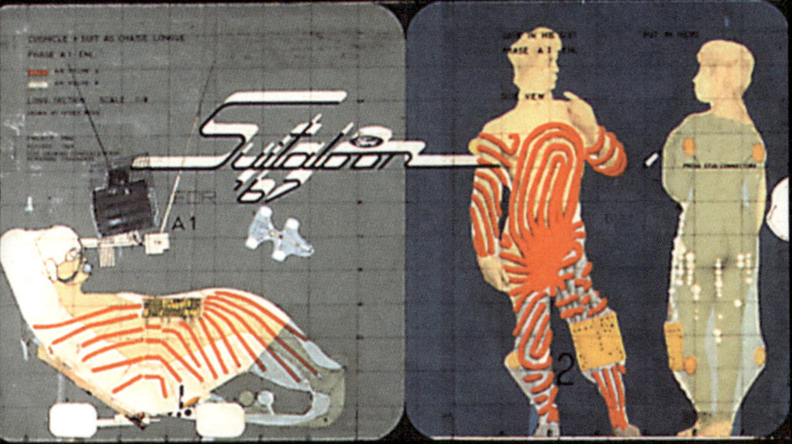

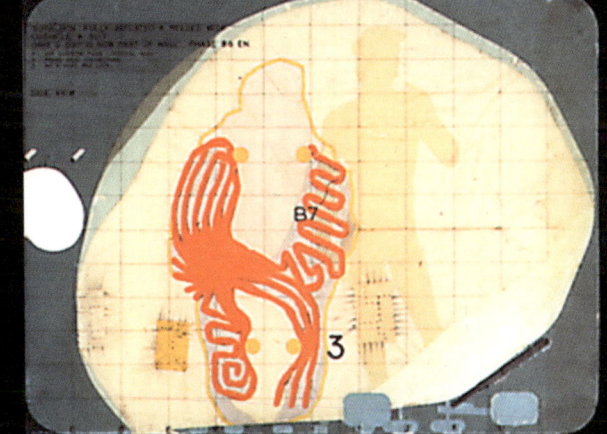

Michael Webb

Peter Cook's Archigram Entr'Acte – 3
FOLKESTONE
1966

Nowadays people – particularly friends or commentators from France, Germany or Scandinavia – constantly refer to 'Folkestone' as a key event. It marked the beginning of a major aspect of our survival – to use the word in its ethical rather than its malarial sense. It is one thing to exchange letters and pamphlets with Hans Hollien, another to have him around; one thing for Reyner Banham to give us the first serious critical support (and critical stimulus), another to have him physically and gregariously present. It exposed us to the beginnings of the long period of love/hate that existed between us and the French and (later) German bodies of Marxist intellectuals who (as we often said amongst ourselves) preached anti-materialism but had a Mercedes parked around the corner. They came to Folkestone and chanted slogans, but never came up with anything as formally whizzy as our stuff! Maybe *that* was the problem.

Claude Parent and Paul Virilio – now each in his own way recognised (in the French pavilion at the Venice Bienale '96) as a key figure in the explosion of urban thinking – were there, in Cardin suits and a Rolls-Royce. At the time they were (like Cedric was in the beginning) slightly grand. The whole European connection, those surprising 300 who ferried, cycled (or Rolls-Royced) over at £3 a crossing direct from Calais to Folkestone, met up with the other 300, mostly from London NW3,

The missing component was Greene and Webb – missing in the sense that they had both gone to teach in the United States, up on the hilltop retreat of VPI where Archigram was so far little known (and therefore no threat). Out of this creative exile came Webb's 'Cushicle' and Greene's 'Living Pod'. The Pod arrived in a box and with its accompanying drawings was a tremendous uplift to the London contingent. The Cushicle, too, confirmed what we had always known, that Mike could sit anywhere – in a hut, a shed, a bedroom – and just explore away. The succinct power of the Cushicle stood beside the 'Furniture Factory' and the 'Sin Centre' as a unique but instantly memorable icon.

A pattern was set. Ron and Warren spent a few years in the USA, David returned, and Mike has lived there ever since. His kids are grown up and are, I suppose, American, though he has retained a wonderfully intact accent as well as an almost forgotten pace of speaking – lost from the English of the Estuary and the Mobile, but which from him authenticates the gradual (and very straight) description of his spatial, geometrical and temporal explorations.

The early 1970s affected Mike's work only slightly: there is of course a certain parody of the American way of life in 'Rent-a-Wall' or 'Dreams Come True', which is dispensed with fairly obviously in the 'Henley' project, which seems to be his fourth classic 'base'. Except for the 'Furniture Factory', they have all been returned-to in several sorties and given successive layers of meaning, exploration, rarification and obsession. In recent years Webb has become a brilliant lecturer, using his slight play at being the English Eccentric as a means (it would seem) to get the audience to slow down and concentrate, to somehow come inside his mind and worry at a point with him.

All this is far from Folkestone, for the event was a rally as much as anything else. Indeed, its 10th anniversary was called 'The Rally' (held at Art Net in London, with 'Folkestone Veteran' badges available to those who attended both events). The making of plastic dresses, the camping on the cliffs – and, I suppose, the French chanting – were essential ingredients of the rhetoric that we had introduced way back in 1961 with the cry 'You can roll out steel ... ANY LENGTH!' In David's challenge lay the invective that shouted 'stop' to all that mimsy English imitation Corbusier as well as the straight reactionary stuff. Historians will probably choose their own preference – the reiterative, monk-like research of Webb's investigations (though himself far from a monk, there is something timeless and detached about him) or the clear markers (*Archigram* 1, IDEA Folkestone, the Archigram exhibiutions at the ICA in 1973 and Vienna 1994) which inevitably, by celebrating loudly, bypass the really gritty aspects of the work.

Within the untidy structure of it all and the questions asked – How did you all add up, if from different schools? How did you/do you correspond with Mike? By the time you had an office, who was actually in there? Did you draw it all yourself/selves? Did Archigram ever really stop (to which those of us who didn't stop drawing would probably say 'No, in a way, no' – there probably lies a giant clue. The strength of Archigram was surely its layers of inconsistent parts, keeping going a continual fascination with each other rather than a statutory obligation to keep in chorus.

Archigram Classic
LIVING POD
David Greene, 1966

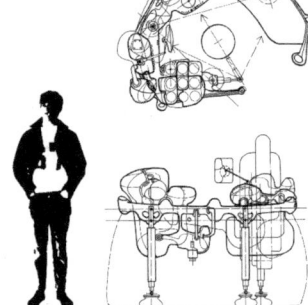

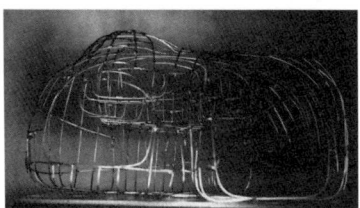

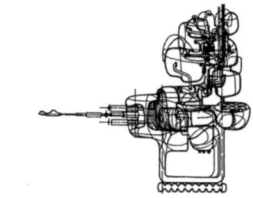

A combination of two passions of Greene: the first towards the idea of the sculpted shell : his enthusiasm for Freidrich Kiesler 'Endless House' which informed Greene's own 'mosque' project (in Archigram 1) and the idea of 'burrowing' explored by Greene in Archigram 2. The second towards the ironic as well as problem solving aspects of gadgetry. The pod is the natural fusion of them both. Yet it can also be regarded as the most sophisticated of the 'capsules' – there are a number of Greene suggestions for the stacking of the pods in a frame structure.

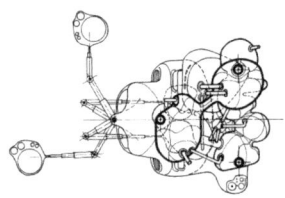

Living Pod

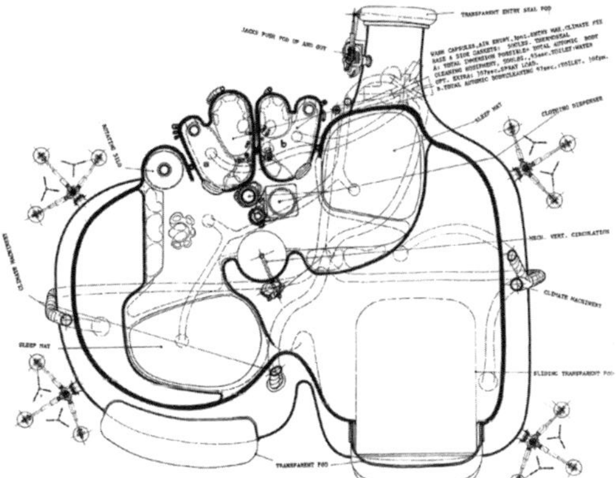

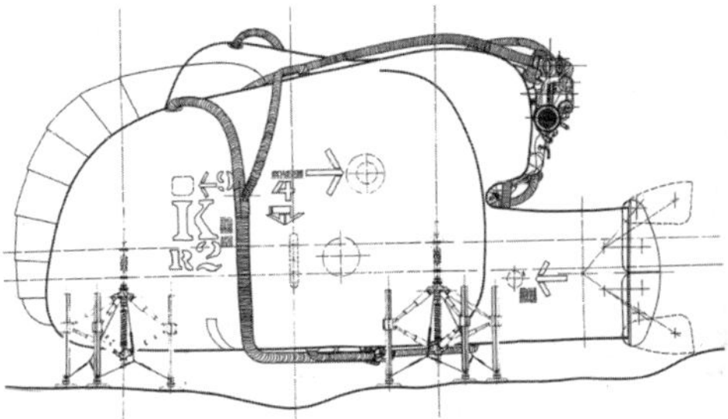

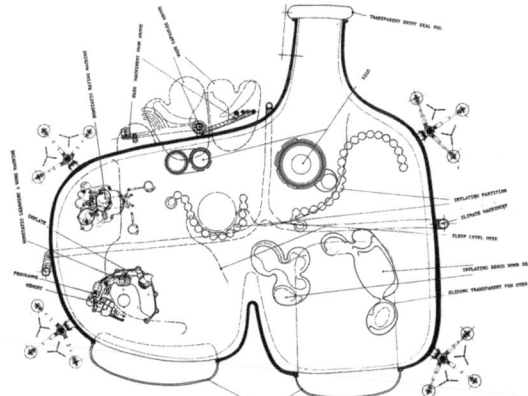
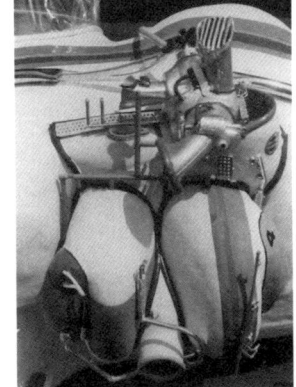

David Greene

Living Pod

David Greene

ARCHIGRAM ROBOTS

In a series of cartoons supporting the 'Control and Choice' dwelling much play is given to the connotation of the robot with the human being. Yet the fascination with the 'servant' role of the robot has to be seen together with its main significance to the Archigram Group: as a key addition to the architect's vocabulary – roof, wall, door, window, robot, floor etc.

The next stage involves the assumption of certain additional roles previously played by columns, screens, walls, enclosures or at least conditions in juxtaposition with facilities so that the idea of 'robotisation' is closely linked to the other ideas of mobility and the gradual melting of architecture.

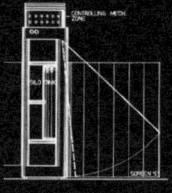
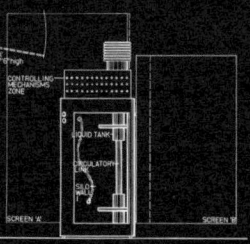

*above right and opposite page: Fred and James, the two robot helpers in the 1990 House
below: the Control and Choice dwelling developing over time. 1990 House and the drawing and model on the next spread correspond roughly to the 1970–5 period*

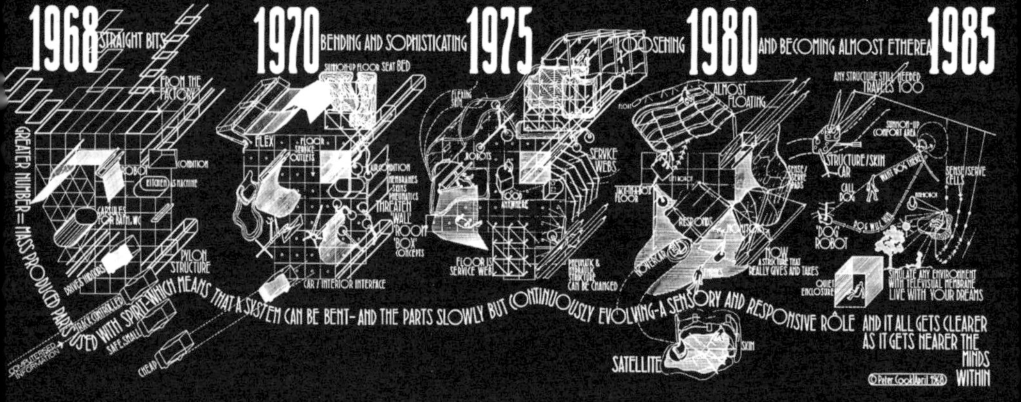

MOBILE PROJECTS

Walking City, *Ron Herron* 1964

If 'Walking City' is the heroic statement of mobilised architecture it represents but the most magnificent audacity of a series of Archigram projects that constantly revolve around flexing, moving, transferring. The origins of this concern are almost certainly related to the overall idea of 'fragmentation'. Making a building like a car, or de-solidifying the 'total element' are allied manoeuvres.

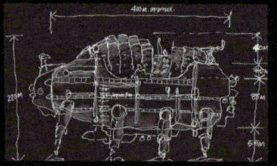
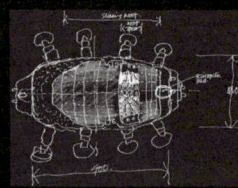
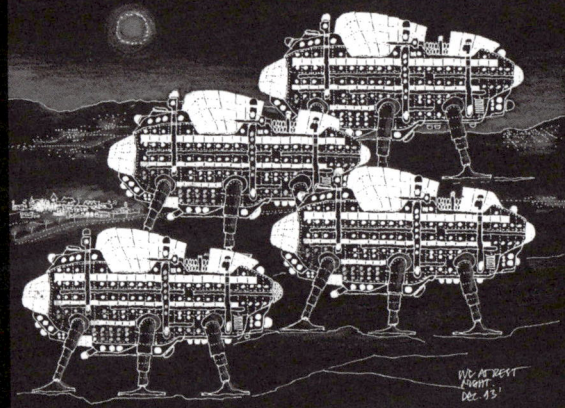
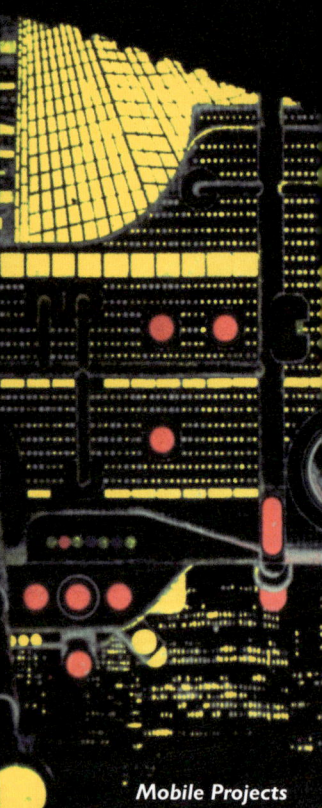

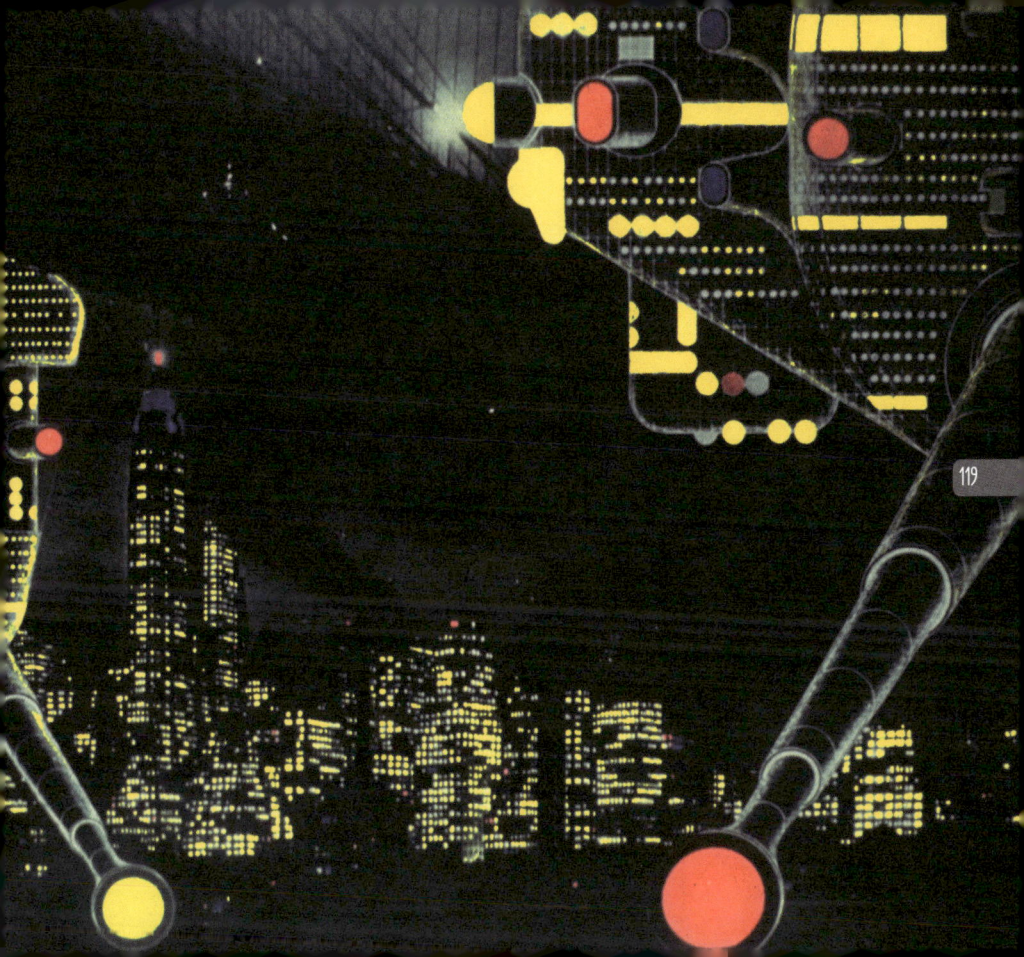

Blow-out Village, *Peter Cook* 1966

The Blow-out Village aimed to combine three aspects of technology together as support for an exploded version of one of our cultural icons 'the village'. Nothing sweet and homely here – the hovercraft, hydraulics and the inflatable are combined. The village is a package that only comes into full fruition when it arrives.

Mobile Projects

121

Peter Cook's Archigram Entr'Acte – 4
LOS ANGELES

Los Angeles really did seem the right place to be. Warren and Ron had been together at UCLA for some months and I was finally (later than anyone else I knew) ready for the USA. Banham had briefed us copiously by way of his 8mm films (that would become the basis for the famous *Four Ecologies* book, but which were so evocative that when I got there I simply had to say: 'but it's exactly like …'). I was to introduce Alan Stanton and Chris Dawson – two of my AA students – to the course that Ron, Arata Isozaki and I were to teach together at UCLA. No wonder that Ron and I were able to develop our respective 'Instant City' projects. In fact the basics for them had already existed in the 'Ideas Circus' and other bits and pieces, but in LA they flourished – if you ran short, for a moment, on inspiration for a city that melted before you, then you could just walk down the street into Westwood.

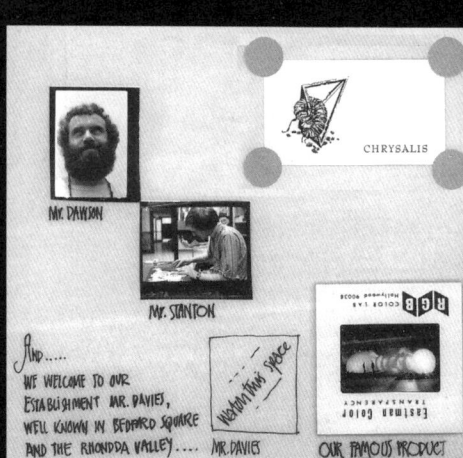

Los Angeles really did seem to stay outside (for quite a while) the piety and rhetoric of the European angst –1968 and all that. To enter the auditorium for the LA version of *Hair* you simply entered the door from the street and you were into the show; the bare bodies and the singing from the roof were no more radical than anything else on Sunset.

The course that we taught was called 'Urban

Isozaki's robots at Osaka

The mirror dome also proposed for Osaka by the 'LA gang'

Design', which gave us the mandate to explore the non-city, ie the *instant* city that we were drawing. Bear in mind that Isozaki would return to make his famous robotised arena in Osaka a year or so later. Remember that Stanton and Dawson would be joined a year later by Mike Davies (also from the AA) and they would create 'Chrysalis' and the 'Myra Breckonridge' Dome. Remember that we would return to elasticate ourselves around such unlikely ground as Monte Carlo and introduce what can only be described as derivatives from 'Instant City', but brought under control and refined.

From time to time – reinforced by repeated visits to Los Angeles and remembering the very special mixture of influences on campus, going to sheds to see acid-head light shows, Sam Francis paintings, Konrad Wachsmann in his laboratory, or just wallowing in the industrial stuff of Long Beach – one cannot help asking whether that city could not have become a very creative base for Archigram. That Gehry and the Morphosis and Moss boys came out of LA seems to suggest that its very distance from Europe – and that *other* Europe that exists somewhere between Harvard and Princeton – is of positive, creative, value.

What actually happened, of course, was the winning of the Monte Carlo competition and the making of an office in London.

Nomad, *Peter Cook* 1968

The Nomad is a follower of Webb's 'Cushicle' on the one hand and the miniaturisation of the 'Village' on the other. Several Archigram projects take on the speculation of 'how much can a man carry that can turn into an environment ?'

Mobile Projects

Ideas Circus, *Peter Cook* 1968

The IDEAS CIRCUS was quite literally created out of the direct experience of the Archigram Group itself going round and doing 'events'. The need for instant enclosures, support structures and the carrying around of special fully-equipped 'carrels' is organised together with a predictive system of locations and ' feeds'. Cedric Price's 'Potteries Thinkbelt' is also another key reference here.

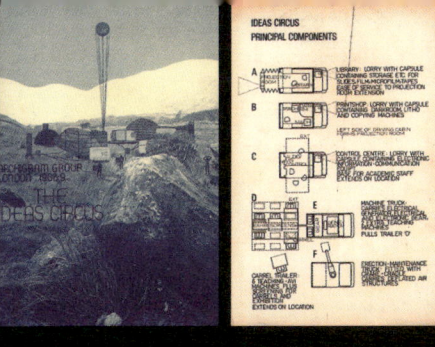
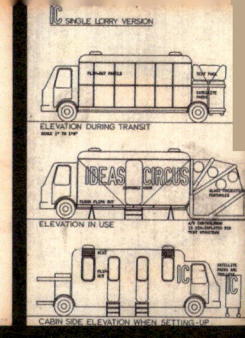

Instant City, *Peter Cook, Dennis Crompton, Ron Herron* 1968

The Cook version of the INSTANT CITY is therefore a direct extension of the Ideas Circus. Elaborated and less concentrated upon the educative aspects of the travelling environment, it anticipated (or simply used the same gear as) the Woodstock Pop Festival. As Ron Herron started to develop a parallel project, he located in Santa Monica, whereas the Cook project remained located in England – despite the fact that several of the drawing were made in Los Angeles !

Mobile Projects

Instant City on the beach at Bournemouth

Mobile Projects

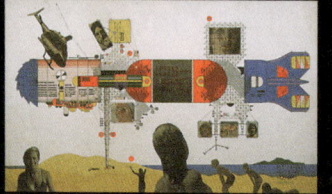
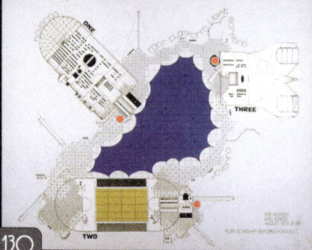

*top two drawings on left and model,
Instant City Airship Deployed, lower two drawings,
Instant City in Santa Monica, Ron Herron 1969–*

Mobile Projects

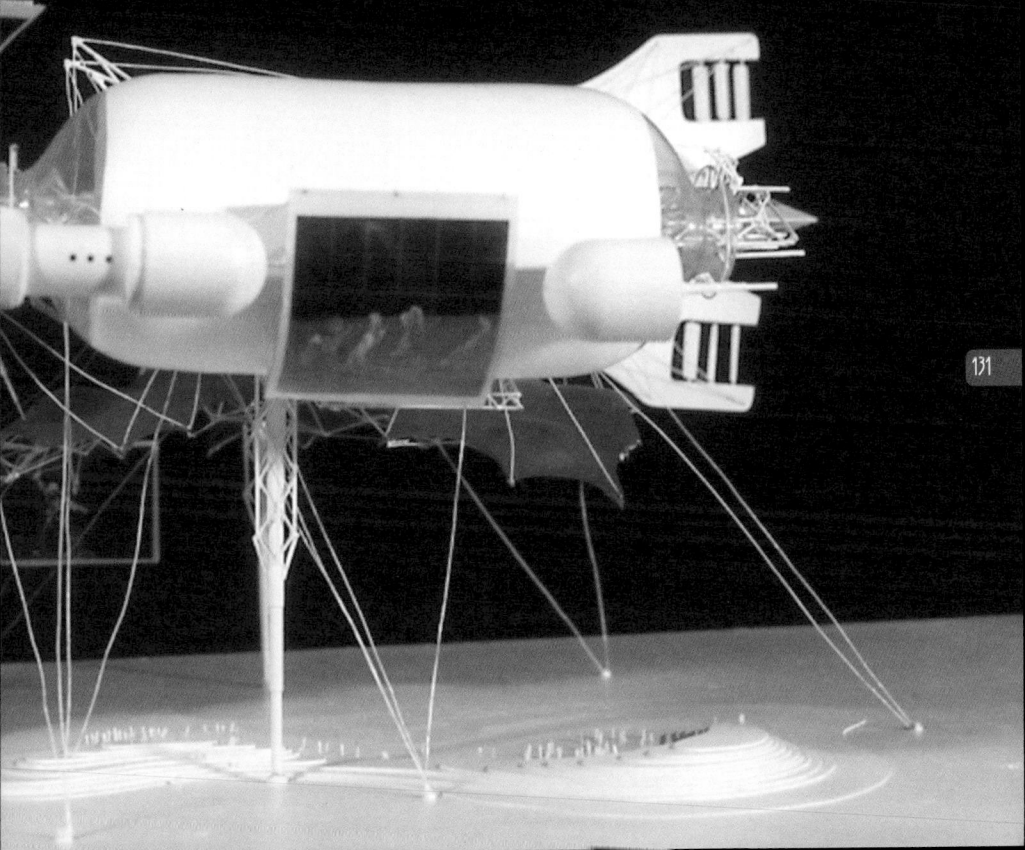

MONTE CARLO – 3 PROJECTS

FEATURES: MONTE CARLO

The Monte Carlo Competition for an entertainments facility was eventually undertaken by eleven offices: preselected through the submission of brochures of work. The most notable fellow-competitor being Riccardo Bofil. Our project was developed in the classical manner: with daily brainstorming sessions in the top studio of the AA (borrowed for the Summer). Cook, Greene and Crompton were joined by Colin Fournier – a recent graduate of the AA – and at a fairly early stage, Frank Newby (the favourite engineer of both Price and Stirling and a participant in 'This is Tomorrow'). Newby gently persuaded the team away from the idea of a rectangular hidden chamber to that of a circle – as a more efficient structural shape. Greene concentrated mostly on the 'park' above and invented the idea of the fully serviced landscape. Cook and Fournier were joined by Ken Allinson and in six weeks the project was ready for 'production'.

In all, fifty-seven sheets of drawings made up the total competition package. Deliberately organised so that six typical (and very different) events could be demonstrated as exploiting the advantages of the fully 'robotised' environment. The mode of drawing was analogous to the principles of the building so that the standard components were

The site as existing and................as proposed

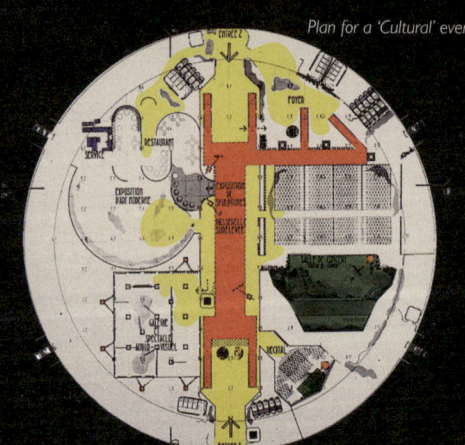

Plan for a 'Cultural' event

Monte Carlo

Banquet

produced as 'stickers' and then moved around and plugged-into the service floor and roof: the form of the space being arranged for the specific event. In other words, Monte Carlo had no architecture – this was to be in the hands of the producer of the show, ringmaster of the Circus… or whoever. 'Architecture as a kit of parts'.

Plan for a 'Banquey

Cultural event

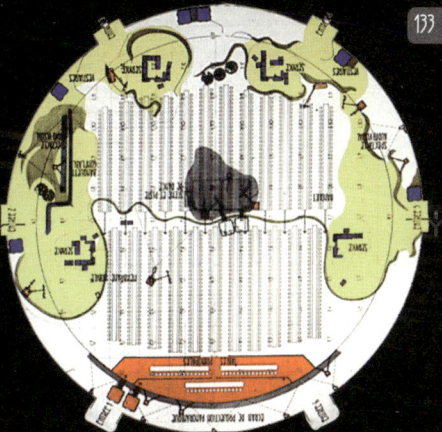

Entrance on the Avenue Princess Grace, and, opposite on arriving at the low-level foyer

Monte Carlo

Whilst working on the detailed design of the Monte Carlo project, Archigram were invited to take part in a second competition. This was for the redevelopment of the Summer Sporting Club. An existing but

Monte Carlo

run-down facility on the beach to the east of our site. We made two proposals for this projects which was to include gambling rooms, a night club, a restaurant and an events space known as the Gala Hall.

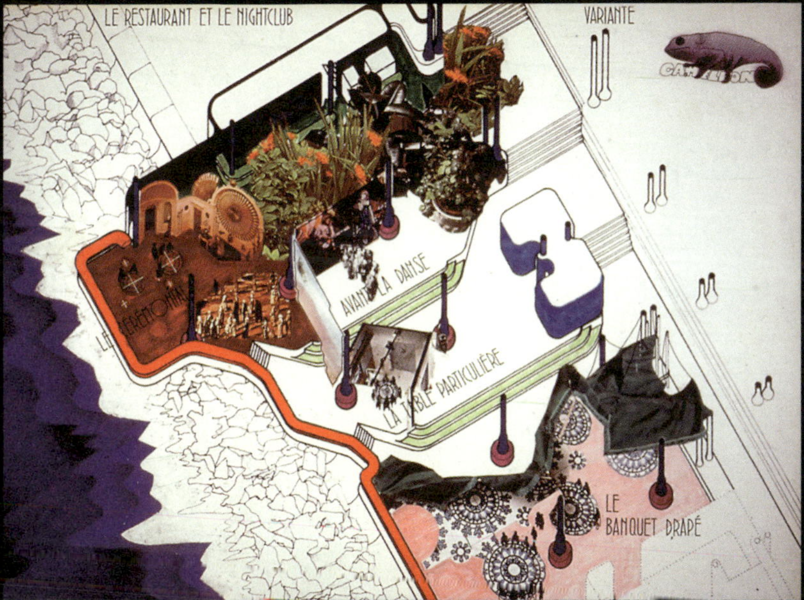

LE RESTAURANT ET LE NIGHTCLUB

VARIANTE

AVANT LA DANSE

LA TABLE PARTICULIÈRE

LE BANQUET DRAPÉ

Peter Cook's Archigram Entr'Acte – 5
ADDHOX

If you have a shop you might as well sell something in it. The choice of Endell Street in Covent Garden was circumstantial – as all such things are. I doubt if we really knew or cared that Covent Garden would become the tourist town that it is now, or thought that if were canny enough to hang on in there we could become real estate barons. No, we were fascinated by the fact that the premises had been the studio (and, by the look of it, the playground) of a famous theatrical photographer. Inevitably and painfully, our own superimposed gadgets and rounded corners overlaid his cherubs and miniaturised cornices. With two or three tiny floors of 'office' and 'workshop' … what to do with the shop?

53 Endell Street, WC2. 01-240-0141

So came about, for only three shows, the gallery 'Addhox'. The first was by the Coop Himmelblau pair. In town to do some things at the AA, Wolf Prix and Helmuth Swicinsky were demonstrably more propitiously chosen as allies than we could ever have realised at the time. Remember that Austria had already spawned Hollien and Pichler, Abraham and St Florian, Haus-Rucker, Domenig and Huth … with Zund-up and Missing Link to follow shortly. Superstudio, Archizoom and 999 already existed in Florence and Clip-Kit and Multimatch were somewhere down the street. But in Himmelblau (though only two guys) there was something more of ourselves. For years they hung on inpushing boundaries, with the circular room at Sielerstatte which is still the core of their office. Like Archigram, they used rhetoric and events, yet did their most serious stuff when apparently sending it (or, rather, pompous architecture) all up.

Imagination seen from Bedford Square, Ron Herron 1989

Frankfurt roof, Cook & Hawley 1987

Coop Himmelblau 1969

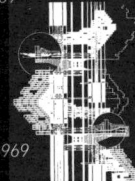
Bernhard Hafner 1969

Wolf Prix 1966-7

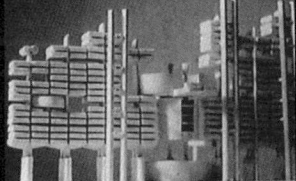

Buper Studio 1969

When asked if Archigram stuff was intended to be built, one often goes into elaborate detail about the scalar accuracy of pieces; one talks about half-step and full-step projects, about sequences of influence. With their permission, I could more usefully point to Himmelblau. At the time of Addhox (1971), Archigram had an office *and* a gallery in which other young experimenters could show. Himmelblau developed an office from which large buildings have emerged. There is no conceptual dividing line. Ron's Imagination building is 95 per cent like the drawings, which are themselves 95 per cent like Archigram drawings. The Cook/Hawley 'mouth' roof in Frankfurt is a straight piece of Archigrammic arm-movement.

Günther Domenig 1966-9

Art Net became, in reality, the much-expanded manifestation of Addhox ... and was in the next street.

To say that this means that Archigram was ready to set up a series of families — Austrian cousins and Japanese nephews and nieces, English clones and a whole system of fragmentations — might be an extravagant claim or, more accurately, an 'add ho(c)x' situation.

Art Net, Colin Rowe ... and ... Bernard Tschumi

Landscape Projects

A number of landscape projects have emerged from 'Archigram': particularly the mysterious 'Botteries', Logplug and Rockplugs (secret service/robotic elements) from David Greene. By contrast Peter Cook's rural projects are all essays in discreet urbanise the Crater City houses 16,000 souls: but you cannot see the single building in which they live because it lines the crater. Similarly, the hedgerow villages are behind the hedgerows.

Foulness Settlements (Q.T.F.S.), Peter Cook 1971

Landscapes

Crater City, Peter Cook 1971

Hedgerow Village, Peter Cook 1972

Orchard Place, Peter Cook 1972

An Experimental Bottery, David Greene 1969

L.A.W.U.N. project number one : BOTTERY

the world's last hardware event'

'The World's Last Hardware Event'

'THE WORLD'S LAST HARDWARE EVENT'

Imagine a landscape and imagine these people sitting here, they are in a Bottery.

Who is sitting where – I mean there are
some people sitting on the ground with a
television set – they are all sitting in a landscape and what you've done – you've cut out pictures and laid them on a landscape – now what would happen if it was the other way round? If you started off with people and the hardware and filled in the space around them – do you think you'd end up with a landscape?

DEFINITIONS: a Bottery is a fully serviced natural landscape.

The Bot: machine-transient in the landscape.

This text is based on the script for a four-screen slide show presented by David Greene and Mike Myers

Bottery

I mean I don't know –
maybe you end up with a big pink blancmange –
something with an antenna in a thousand-miles-wide pie-dish.

Here is another picture.

Imagine this man – but he is not sitting here fishing
he is sitting here on the top of a building
and he's got his socks on the end of his line….

…drying in the updraught
or it could be a security guard in which
the television is monitoring the front gate
and the fishing rod is a microphone …

or he could be dead

yes, he probably is.

But the picture of this man by the river collects together
most of the images and influences that produce this project –
– the transient specialised environment.

David Greene

Which is the more transient / specialised – the landscape or the television?

This environment is made possible by the development
of sophisticated portable hardware – such as portable TVs,
pocket calculators etc, etc.

What do you think –
give me some hardware that isn't sophisticated –
give me a piece of unsophisticated hardware –

a leather shoe,
a saw,
a tap,
a candle –

I don't agree with you at all –
I think they are incredibly sophisticated those things –
it depends on you.

anyway, here he is – sitting with his ice box

sitting with his ice box?

Yes –

where is his ice box?

World's Last Hardware Event

and his car is behind him

he is sitting with his TV/ice box/car behind him, all neat,
got his own scene going for him, and yet it can all be taken away –
and when it's gone,
there is nothing to show that it was there at all
     except a small amount of
  crushed grass and perhaps a tyre-track, a footprint –

– so it's all invisible in a way
– a temporary place,   retained perhaps permanently in the memory –
        an architecture that exists only with reference to time.

IT IS THE DIMENSION OF ABSENCE THAT IS TO BE FOUND –

Locally Available World Unseen Networks – **L.A.W.U.N.**

L.A.W.U.N. – project number one

journey into space, interior space

David Greene

HELLO – I'M A VOICE ON A MACHINE

and so am I –

(and me)

with an invitation to penetrate an idea. Ideas are like houses – all houses have front doors. Think of me as a front door.

It's funny that for some years now time has been
an important influence in the arts – that is except in
architecture, apart from nominal and superficial concessions
to movement and communication. Perhaps architects knew all along
that if they come to grips with time they might be right out of a job.

>	I have a desire for the built environment to allow me to do my own thing.

>	more and more people want to determine their own parameters of behaviour –
>	they want to decide how they shall behave, whether it's play, working, loving –
>	people are less and less prepared to accept imposed rules and patterns of behaviour –
>	doing your own thing is important;

People are becoming more interested in people and reality – rather than in feeding mythical systems
(Warren Chalk)

World's Last Hardware Event

Unfortunately however in terms of doing your own thing
architecture is clearly not working

                          It is important to note that the trends in society and
                          technology are searching for flexibility and versatility –
                          specialisation is dead –

in the building world the idea of the multipurpose shed
plays lip service to this observation;
the idea of non-specialised systems and architecture begin to interact:

        the plane that jumps – the boat that walks – the tie that is a pen

        machines that talk,
            doors that open

think of yourself as a room –
    think of yourself as for one specific purpose:
        it isn't viable any more – that's obvious

    everything is mixed up –
    it's all fragmented;
        as a room I'm just as confused as you are as a person;

Unless of course I'm an architect –
    in which case I still seem to think that building types exist
        and it is useful to give rooms specific purposes

                on my drawings

David Greene

I have a desire for the environment to be invisible,
in order that I may be free
from the pornography known as buildings.

One of the most interesting observables for architects about some recent sculpture
is that it takes great care not to disturb the existing environment
and in fact draws from its situation and feeds on all the ongoing events and processes
that any particular site contains.
Jack Burnham describes it as
'using the untapped energy and information network of the day-to-day environment'

Both sets of pictures, the fisherman by the river and
the landscapes involve the temporary placing of bits
of hardware in a natural scene
and their ultimate removal.

About this project Smithson writes:

'IT IS THE DIMENSION OF ABSENCE THAT IS TO BE FOUND.'

So maybe you might say that
the development of portable hardware
produces an architecture of absence –
you've got to know about when it's not there as well as when it is there.

World's Last Hardware Event

Cowboy international nomad hero.

It used to seem to be a nice idea
    to carry your environment around with you –
        space-man, cushicle, suitaloon etc –
but that can be as much of a drag as having it stuck in one place.

Cowboy was probably one of the most successful
carriers of his own environment
because his hardware needs –
mug, saddle, bedroll matches etc –
were low and because his prime mover, HORSE, selected its
own fuel as a fairly self-sufficient animal robot.

The ranch was his oasis, his base.

    Modern nomads need sophisticated servicing –
    Howard Johnson understands this –
    and in the Bottery this is achieved
        by the technique of calling it up wherever you are –
        it's delivered by robots –
        it's anarchy and it's hardware supported
        until it's under the skin –
        or in the mind.

David Greene

Marshal McLuhan has said that the planet earth
can be understood now
as a piece of sculpture

                in the galaxies

even simple men understand that

the Bottery is part of the idea of space park earth –

Here's Keymatic, a familiar piece of
(purchasable) hardware, part of a long
line of crude domestic robots such as
dishwasher, mixer, central heating etc,
etc –

The thing about Keymatic that's nice
is the system of programming
which is done by a simple
plastic plate –

Every house now contains crude robots,
everybody wants a house full of robots,
but no one wants it to look like a house full of robots –
so why not forget about the house altogether and just have a garden
                                  and a collection of robots?

World's Last Hardware Event

Hello, hello – I'm another voice – but I'm more than a voice, I'm an interruption – I'm interrupting your conversation to raw attention to the picture that you are now looking at, of the mobot on the lawn with dog sitting in front of it. I'm a voice to suggest that you try and work out tthe difference is between the mobot and the dog – if you owned both, which one would you care more about?

    Maybe you paid more for one or the other,

        maybe one can get sicker than the other,

        maybe you talk to one and not the other,

        maybe one does more for you than the other,

        maybe one is less dangerous to your kids than the other,

        maybe you take one on holiday and leave the other behind and

        maybe when you get back from holiday

            you get more anxious about one than the other –

David Greene

```
No good presentation is good without an interview — so I think we should have an
interview now and here is the first question:
— a lot of people think that the word robot is a nasty word, it means mindless,
automatic, and it corresponds to people's image of a terrible future — but I know
you don't have this view of the word robot
```

> *No. We must not attribute human characteristics to the machine*

```
When you say 'robot', you don't mean it as a put down do you?
```

> No, I don't. Most people's lives are full of robots.
> They use robots, anyway — the car is only a kind of a robot —
> a radio, record player;
> the electric toothbrush is a robot that saves you moving your hand up and down
> — I use 'robot' in that sense;

```
It is important to remove the feeling in the audience's mind
that 'robot' is — is like dangerous or threatening because of
the prevailing condition recently to think of it like that.
```

> Yes, I don't know how you remove that,
> I suppose that's the image in the comic of the robot,
> the 'Dr Who' image of the robot

```
but the people who are most afraid of robots
are the people who are most like them!
```

> You bet —

```
that was a good interview —
                                 thank you
```

World's Last Hardware Event

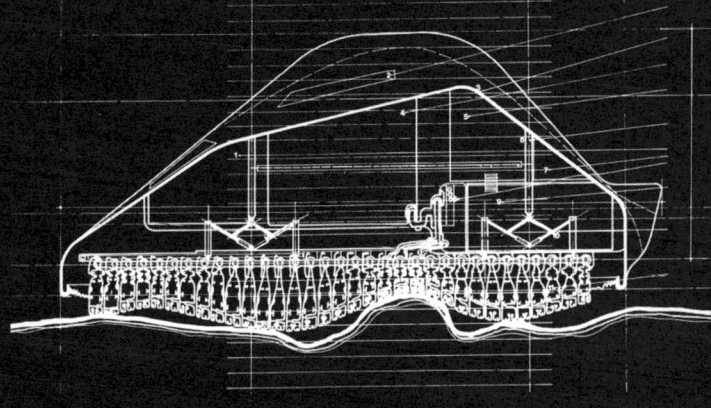

Here's a typical cross section of a robot which would be roaming in a Bottery, and obviously the sort of service that the robot would deliver would vary from Bottery to Bottery. You can see the basic components of the module which are a power unit which drives it along in this sort of 'worm-like' motion, a cover and then a frame inside to contain different modules – for instance you might imagine a park that was specifically catering for people who are learning – the sort of person that you now call a student – in which case a module might deliver a certain kind of projection device or it might deliver a certain package of memory information or it might deliver something to sit on or something, or sometimes it might even deliver certain kinds of food and they would be contained as modules underneath this overall skin –

How do you send for it?

Well you send for it with this call-up device which is a small homing device…

David Greene

about the size of a ball-point pen – on the
top you'd have a selection switch to select
the module that you want to be delivered
and you just press the button and it would
come to you and it probably also displays
the time that it would take the Bot to arrive –

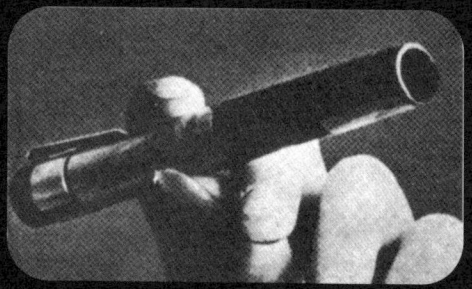

I think it is realy important not to think of this as science fiction fantasy
but as a piece of feasible architecture, possible now –

Well, technically it's feasible – whether it's desirable is another
argument – but this project wasn't about that, it was about setting a
pilot-study and the area for the pilot-study where these Bots would be
experimented with was fairly close to Poole harbour. It's shown on this
map here. It's a little-used area of considerable natural beauty and
includes a number of heaths – a country sort of heath land and water
land. It would be possible to study the nature of the interface between
man and the Bot. In other words – how can we use them and also the
actual performance of the Bot itself – more efficient power modules
and more efficient homing devices and miniaturisation of enclosure-
systems and any other services.

World's Last Hardware Event

This is a base and servicing bay, a prefabricated construction with an outer shell which would be designed to blend in with the local scene – the style shown here is from the country cottage range.

Number two in the picture, Combot, brings to your side out of the bluebells a way into your own secret mind or selects, out of the world's transmitted invisible pictures and sounds, your own pattern of information and shows it to you on your shirt or on a screen. This is a brief community of people gathered together in the world park – they called up their Bots. The gathering is only related to time – tomorrow, in half an hour, next week, it will all change. There will be nothing remaining to indicate that it was there and the natural scene will remain unchanged. This small instant village will exist only in the memories of the people who were there and in the information memory of the robot – an invisible village, an architecture existing only in time.

David Greene

This couple, still living in their nice house, turn on with Combots in the evenings. However, they're already wondering why they need any furniture and have their Combot networked into their office in town and don't need to commute anymore –
    maybe next year they can move into a grass field somewhere.

One of the questions often asked about this kind of project is, how do you make it happen? In this project as well as in the experimental landscape venture it can be made to happen through the marketing of robots and their gradual absorption into our everyday live – just as frozen food has made a cooker in a way less necessary, less useful and yet even more desirable as a tool for creativity in the kitchen, so increasingly sophisticated and efficient domestic robots will make the permenant living base or 'house' less useful and will open up new areas and meanings for the word 'home'.

Locally Available World Unseen Network –

L.A.W.U.N. means the striving after basic objectives –
    doing your own thing without disturbing the events of the existing scene and in
    a way which is invisible because it involves no formal statement and
    because it is related to time –
        may or may not be there at any given point in time…

World's Last Hardware Event

What does that mean?

Ah, it means basically three things.

Firstly, time.
You have an architecture which is related to time …
if you look at the man by the river – he is only there for a given period of time
and when he is not there, there is no record of him being there.
He is not going to leave a hut there with his boots in and his television set.

The second thing is that it involves no formal statement.
When he lays out his hardware he doesn't lay it out according to any prescribed
aesthetic rules, he doesn't line up the television with the back leg of the chair and
make sure that his fishing rod is at right angles to the bumper on the car,
so it involves no formal aesthetic statement,

and lastly, it's an attempt to describe a way of doing things and disturbing the
existing environment as little as possible.
You don't bring in bulldozers, you don't alter trees,
you try to leave things as much as they are and
work more guerilla fashion within what exists there already,
and that really is the intention of the Bottery.

By taking these three basic objectives and adding to it a technology of
robots, this kind of invisible guerilla environment may be made to work.

Is that like trying to walk over snow without leaving any tracks?

Only in the sense that the tracks are related to time …

and they disappear when the snow falls?

David Greene

ARCHIGRAM
WELCOME TO NEW YORK

William Menking

Welcome to New York, New York. No, not New York, New York in Las Vegas – the theme park as city – but New York, New York in New York – the city as theme park. Here you can visit recently created adult theme lands: Soho and Chelsea (Artland), Battery Park City (Financialfantasyland), Chinatown (Foodadventureland), and the 'wild' Lower East Side (Realestatefrontierland). Since the transformation of a once-lively 14-block-square district of artists' lofts and commercial markets in lower Manhattan into a themed 'South Street Seaport' shopping 'experience', New York is increasingly being zoned into such sanitised districts.[1] To visit real – which is to say, not re-invented urban fantasy, you will need to leave Manhattan island and venture out to areas like the dishevelled and disinvested Coney Island neighbourhood in Brooklyn.

A short distance from your midtown Manhattan hotel room you can visit the latest and most fantastic urban themed land –Times Square. That's where Disney Corporation's Imagineering Research and Development Unit and local architects and politicians have created the city's newest entertainment experience in the renovated New Amsterdam Theater. Here, in what was once the 'Crossroads of the World', you will also find ventures similar to Madame Tussaud's Waxworks; Cinema Ride, a flight simulation experience; scores of ersatz themed restaurants and a soon-to-open Planet Hollywood Hotel with its own themed rooms. Finally, in the heart of the district, Virgin Records has opened what it

A shorter version of this text appears in *Archigram symposium zur Ausstelung*, Ritter Verlag 1997.
All Archigram citations in this text come from *A Guide to Archigram 1961–74* (Academy Editions, London 1994), published on the occasion of the Archigram exhibition at the Kunsthalle, Vienna.

1 'South Street Seaport Plan' in advertising supplement to *The New York Times*, 1984; quoted in M Christine Boyer: *Manhattan Manners* (MIT Press, Cambridge, Mass 1994).

calls the world's largest record store in a huge Piranesi-style shopping mall.

You may remember Times Square from ten years ago, when a single block from Broadway to Eighth Avenue along 42nd Street had ten enormous movie palaces, some open 24 hours a day. This was where many young African Americans from Harlem went to the cinema, for their neighbourhood, despite a population of 200,000, had no movie theatres. The block also contained countless inexpensive all-night restaurants and fast-food stands, XXX-rated book stores, peep shows and sex shops, and pinball arcades – the 'dark grey areas' that Archigram claimed 'all cities required'.[2] Spilling onto its sidewalks were executives from midtown skyscrapers, workers from the adjacent garment district, and elegantly dressed theatre patrons. As one of the city's most authentic spectacles, 42nd Street was the very epitome of Archigram's notion of 'messy vitality'.[3]

This 'messiness', unfortunately, led to 42nd Street's undoing.[4] Real estate developers, who had long coveted this valuable stretch of midtown property, joined together in 1987 with city politicians to create 'The 42nd Street Development Corporation'.[5] This public/private entity hoped to transform the street – which they claimed was a 'sleazy' and 'underutilized' area of the city – into a sleek extension of the adjacent corporate office district.[6]

In 1989, the theatres were condemned, the young African-Americans were sent back to Harlem, and Philip Johnson was commissioned to design a series of massive skyscrapers that he claimed were 'deconstructive'.[7] However, the office market collapsed the following year and the project was put on hold. Except for a single hot-dog stand (now closed), an XXX-rated

2 Peter Cook, The Living City (1963), p. 76.

3 Ibid, p. 74.

4 Ibid.

5 *42 Street Now*, New York State Development Corporation and New York State Economic Development Corporation, 1993.

6 Ibid, p. 4.

7 'The New Times Square', *New York Times*, 30 October 1989.

William Menking

book store and theatre, the city was stuck with a deserted block, a mere remnant of what Lawrence Alloway might have had in mind when he spoke of a 'symbol thick scene, crisscrossed with the tracks of human activity'.[8]

The Development Corporation then commissioned Robert A M Stern to 're-animate' the abandoned block.[9] Stern presented an urban design plan, or marketing scheme, that would decorate the facades of the existing historic buildings with layers of advertising signs that replicate or recall Broadway's history as the 'Great White Way'. Stern asserted that his plan, which excluded skyscrapers, would make 42nd Street look 'noisy, historically layered ... unplanned ... bold and brash', exactly what the street had been before it was condemned.[10] It should be pointed out that Stern's 're-animated' new street is what property speculators call a 'tax payer', ie a holding action until the market rebounds for Johnson-like skyscrapers.

Well, what does Archigram have to tell us about contemporary 'situations' such as 42nd Street? Are their paper concepts still relevant to the current transformation of our old centralised and heterogeneous cities? Can the lads from London help us to avoid mistakes like the one New York is making?

Although 'personal environments' like 'Suitiloons', 'Gasket Homes' and 'Expendable Place Pads' may be entirely credible in today's world of virtual reality, they are only partial solutions for everyday life.[11] We cannot look to Archigram's 'Independent City Modules', 'Seaside Bubbles', 'Plug-In Cities' or Ebenezer Howard-like 'Underwater Cities' for help with today's centre city.[12] Their notion of the city as a series of independent quarters or zones similar to the human brain – 'a collection of cells with an extraordinary high concentration of absolutely essential functions and energy' – seems,

8 Lawrence Alloway: 'The Independent Group: Postwar Britain and the Aesthetics of Plenty' in *The Independent Group: Postwar Britain and the Aesthetics of Plenty* (Cambridge, Mass. 1990), p. 49.
9 42nd Street Now, p. 5.

10 'Rethinking 42d St. For the Next Decade', real estate section of *New York Times*, p. 6.

11 *A Guide to Archigram 1961–74* (Academy Editions, London 1994), p.182.
12 Ibid.

Welcome to New York

30 years on, to lead us to the zoned and controlled spaces of 'Garden City' suburbs, corporate campuses and shopping malls.

In fact, the same political and property development forces that are malling 42nd Street are also attempting to turn it into an 'Independent Module'' using a state chartered entity called a Business Improvement District. These BIDs employ underpaid private security forces, sanitation services etc to create privatised spaces modelled on sanitised 'Garden Cities'. Furthermore, the service workers tending these privileged areas go home to their '(Un)-Plugged' neighbourhoods, or 'Bubbles', where there is little or no security, sanitation or decent schools.

We might instead reconsider Archigram's collages of an oil platform in Trafalgar Square, 'Tuned Suburb' of 1968, or the 'Instant City' programmes of 1970.[13] These 'Urban Action Tune-Ups' offer the possibility of preserving the historic fabric and space of the city while infiltrating 'events, displays and educational programmes into its spaces.'[14] The city, Peter Cook reminds us, 'lives equally in its past, the present where we are and the future'.[15] But Americans, sadly, seem disillusioned with the present and seem to have lost all hope in the future. As Disney's new 'Main Street', 42nd Street, is being redesigned or refurbished by Robert Stern as a Beaux Arts pastiche of historic signs, what urban historian Christine Boyer calls the 'represented image of the city ... that manipulate[s] scenery, ornament and facades to underscore the sentiment of their play ... not the real thing'.[16] However much Stern claims his plan recontextualises the city, he is simply creating another festival marketplace, devoid of the social dynamic that made Times Square an authentically vibrant 'situation'. Stern intends his proposal to be fun, but lacking Archigram's critique and intelligence, it is simply a 'manipulated recreation of a city' – not the real thing.[17]

13 Ibid, chapter '1970'.

14 Peter Cook, op. cit, p. 77.
15 Ibid.

16 From an interview I conducted with Christine Boyer for a 'Museum-In-Progress' article in the *Wien Standard*, 15 March 1966.

17 Ibid.

William Menking

Of course, Archigram has been criticised for being too accepting of expendable architecture and consumer culture. Kenneth Frampton accuses them of raging utopianism, and 'furthering the domain of an optimized technology'.[18] However, like the Independent Group, their acceptance of 'space-age commodities' is understandable in the austerity of post-war Britain, which had little or no experience with a consumer culture of disposable objects.[19] It is easy to find fault with their research into the milieu of commercial mass culture from the point of view of a modernist rationalist perspective. What Dan Graham points out about American pop artists seems to apply equally to groups like Archigram, Superstudio, Ant Farm, Hans Rucker and early Coop Himmelblau. In his essay 'Art in Relation to Architecture/Architecture in Relation to Art', Graham asserts that pop art 'appears to equivocate in its attitudes towards commercialized mass culture, even adopting some its conventions and sentiments'.[20] But he goes on to argue that 'European leftist critics, particularly those investigating architecture, unconsciously equate mass culture with fascist irrationalism, seeing rationalist socialism as both a negation of degraded mass culture and as the only constructive solution to the problems it confronts.' In other words, they see 'present-day American society in terms of Europe in the 1930s'.[21] According to Graham the critique of this 'leftist-theoretical approach' is blinded to the possibilities inherent in architectural research entering into the field of popular mass culture.

Archigram, perhaps under the influence of Reyner Banham and Cedric Price, and with the example of the Independent Group, were among the first to realise that high modernism claimed to be above the cultural domination of these new forms, that architecture and advertising were identical, and that market and media forces

18 Kenneth Frampton: *Modern Architecture: A Critical History* (Thames & Hudson, London 1980), p. 281.

19 Ibid, p. 283.

20 Dan Graham: 'Art in Relation to Architecture/Architecture in Relation to Art', in *Rock My Religion: Writings and Art Projects, 1965–1990*, ed. Brian Wallis (MIT Press, Cambridge, Mass., 1993), p. 230.

21 Ibid, p. 231.

gave the work a different meaning, one beyond the architect's control. Today, which magazine a new building appears in matters as much as the use to which the building is put. Archigram, although working in a different context, realised this about architecture thirty-five years ago, and this is perhaps their most important legacy. Further, the entire anti-establishment youth culture that developed in the 1960s in Europe and America was indeed just as naive as Archigram. It was blind to the contradictions of a future of unlimited leisure in which, as the *Situationist International* pointed out, 'each individual might construct a life, just as in the old world a few privileged artists had constructed their representations of what life could be'.[22] But without this naiveté, the student movements of the 1960s would have been sucked into the boring certainties of professional standards or the easy conventions of liberal political discourse.

I cannot remember when I first became aware of Archigram. It may be that by the time I reached the Berkeley architecture school at the University of California in the late 1960s they were simply in the cultural air that included Fillmore Auditorium posters, Merry Prankster handbills and the SDS broadsheets that were pasted onto the school walls. But students in those years realised that Archigram, like these other cultural phenomena, stood for possibilities and protest.

But something else needs to be pointed out about Archigram. Reread Warren Chalk's post-1968 critique of 'the piped environment of car-crazy LA', which he claimed had 'outlived its usefulness'.[23] Archigrammers, in fact, may have grown and changed their position, or may even have wanted it both ways, but as Peter Cook has written, they always stood 'for a passionately democratic respect for the competing discourses of urban culture' and for the power of their group to 'propose individual or competing notions'.[24]

22 Greil Marcus: Lipstick Traces: A Secret History of the 20th Century (Harvard University Press, Cambridge, Mass., 1989), p. 51.

23 Warren Chalk: Up the Down Ramp (1968), p. 258.

24 Peter Cook: Our Belief in the City... (1963), p. 69.

William Menking

In short, they changed with the times, especially after 1968, without compromising their critique. How much more exciting this notion is as a possibility than the calculated Beaux Arts fantasies or privatised neighbourhoods of contemporary New York.

Americans should take an interest in Archigram, not only because Archigram's critique is predicated on issues still important to the American city, but also because they simply thought and made drawings instead of compromising. Although Kenneth Frampton criticises Archigram's drawings as a 'projection of images in ... inaccessible terms', there is another way to look at their work. Liane Lefaivre has pointed out that groups like Archigram 'used the language of architecture to challenge the stylistic and social bulldozing carried out by the dominant architectural trend of the time'.[25] This is especially important, given that American architects and urbanists today are faced with an economy similar to the one that confronted Archigram in the 1960s. Younger practitioners, many of them former students of Peter Cook and Archigram, are using the same critical strategies to 'crash the gates of today's accepted formal vocabularies by incorporating into their architectural designs unconventional references to the urban context'.[26] Today, the economy (and much of the architecture profession must be held partly responsible) seems to dictate that architecture is a luxury it can hardly afford. American practitioners today build less than 15 per cent of all new buildings. As in the 1960s, drawing (today, computer imaging) increasingly becomes an end in itself, rather than simply the means to build. Further, many of Archigram's proposals feature infrastructure improvements to the existing city, and this could not be more important for the younger generation of students now coming out of architecture school. It will be the challenge of this generation to rebuild the infrastructure

25 Liane Lefaivre, 'Dirty Realism in European Architecture Today', *Design Book Review* (Berkeley, California, Winter 1989), p. 17.

26 Ibid.

Welcome to New York

of our decaying cities; let us hope they give us cities that are as much fun as those projected by the young Archigrammers.

Finally, Archigram's fantastic and playful yet profound critique of the accepted norms of architecture and urban planning practice is not directed against the promises of modernism, in which they continue to believe, but, rather, against their post-World War Two alignment with development, profits and lack of fun. Earlier modernists, such as Le Corbusier and Ray and Charles Eames, were every bit as involved in the utopian technology of their day as the Archigrammers in the first cybernetic revolution. Clearly, ample precedents exist for Archigram's pop contextualism.

Archigram would probably disagree with my belief in master planning. But we would both celebrate 'irreverent play' and Peter Cook's claim for the 'intensity and vibration of metropolitan life … as somehow more conducive to all the great positives: creativeness, emancipation, involvement and enlightenment' – in other words, the modernist ideals. Had we trusted Archigram's 'messy vitality' and celebration of 'urban disorder … as found', 42nd Street would still be authentic, not a Disney 'Main Street' that's 'hopelessly bland, upbeat and robot like', to borrow from *The New York Times*' recent review of Disney's musical *Beauty and the Beast*, now playing daily at the New Amsterdam Theater on 42nd Street.

And yet the situation is not irretrievable. For, like Disney's suburban theme parks, which are built on concrete pads above an underground city for its workers and the flow of detritus, the subway still rumbles under Disney New York. This monument to the vitality of a truly public urban social space is something Archigram would understand. I am sure there is an old 42nd Street somewhere in the depths of the 'Walking City'.

William Menking